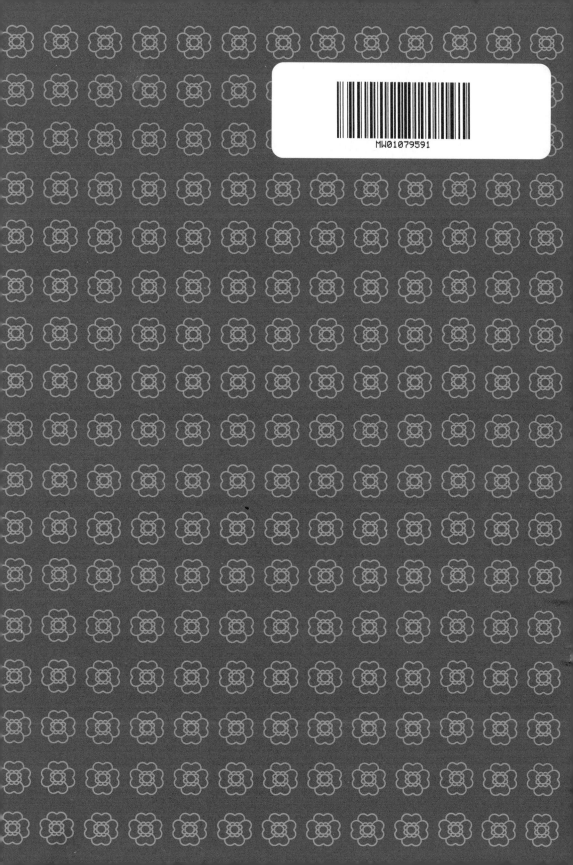

하기쉬운한국요리

KOREAN
MADE EASY

AN HACHETTE UK COMPANY
WWW.HACHETTE.CO.UK

First published in Great Britain in 2024 by
Kyle Books, an imprint of Octopus Publishing Group Limited
Carmelite House
50 Victoria Embankment
London EC4Y 0DZ
www.octopusbooks.co.uk

ISBN: 9781804191804

Distributed in the US by Hachette Book Group, 1290 Avenue of the
Americas, 4th and 5th Floors, New York, NY 10104

Distributed in Canada by Canadian Manda Group, 664 Annette St.,
Toronto, Ontario, Canada M6S 2C8

Publisher: Joanna Copestick
Junior Commissioning Editor: Samhita Foria
Design: Yasia Williams
Cover Design: Evi-O Studio
Food Styling: Jake Fenton, Henrietta Clancy (pages 50, 52, 56, 107, 154)
Props Styling: Max Robinson, Alexander Breeze (pages 50, 52, 56, 107, 154)
Photography: Louise Hagger, Teo Della Torre (page 7)
Production: Emily Noto

Printed and bound in China
10 9 8 7 6 5 4 3 2 1

MIX
Paper | Supporting
responsible forestry
FSC
www.fsc.org   FSC® C008047

하기쉬운한국요리

KOREAN
MADE EASY

SE JI HONG

아침 점심 저녁

SIMPLE RECIPES TO MAKE
FROM MORNING TO MIDNIGHT

K

CONTENTS

☺ **SEJI'S PLAYLIST** ♡ ⏮ ▶ ⏸ ⏭ ⋯

Feel the groove while you cook the recipes in this book – scan the QR code to listen in to Seji's specially crafted playlist.

Hi! I'm Seji ☺

As a self-confessed foodie, my passion is crafting food that brings pure joy to those who taste it. For me, cooking is more than merely mixing ingredients together to make a tasty meal. It's a means of connecting with people, of sharing stories and experiences, and of creating nostalgic moments. In fact, I believe nostalgia is the secret ingredient that elevates any meal to new, delectable heights. Whether I'm in the kitchen experimenting with new recipes or at the dining table surrounded by loved ones, I always strive to create culinary experiences that bring people together in a celebration of food, love and life.

Growing up in South Korea, I was immersed in a rich culinary culture that instilled in me a deep appreciation for cooking. As a child, I spent countless hours in the kitchen with my grandma, learning how to make traditional dishes, such as kimchi from her hometown of Gwangju (see Chapter 1), Cold Spicy Noodles (see page 61) and Doenjang Crab Soup (see page 77). At the same time, my mother's innovative, Western-inspired dishes, such as Gochujang Butter Bucatini (see page 147) and Korean Spicy Fried Chicken (see page 106), added to my culinary curiosity.

Moving to London as a student, I found myself surrounded by a diverse array of cuisines. Inspired by this eye-opening experience, I plucked up the courage to introduce Korean dishes and flavours to close friends. It wasn't long before I was regularly hosting home parties for my friends, where I prepared modern Korean cuisine that was close to my heart. Through word of mouth, these parties became popular, leading to the launch of Bombom supper clubs. Here I served authentic Korean cuisine, alongside some dishes to which I added my own creative twist. Over time, supper-club attendees began enquiring about the sauces I was using, which resulted in me creating my own line of sauces under the name Bombom Market. Through all of this, I developed an archive of dependable Korean recipes that I return to time and time again – which I'm now sharing with you in this book!

Whether it's making classic Korean dishes or putting a modern spin on them, I always infuse my food with authenticity. True to both the London dining scene and Seoul food trends, all my recipes focus on a laid-back cooking style with an array of distinctive but easy-to-make dishes using seven key ingredients. I'd like them to become your regular go-to recipes for an easy Korean meal. Think of this book as your shortcut to Korean flavours.

Enjoy, Seji

A BIT ABOUT KOREAN FOOD & CULTURE
MORNING TO MIDNIGHT: BREAKFAST, LUNCH & DINNER

In Korean culture, the practice of enjoying three daily meals isn't just about nourishing the body; it's a way to connect with others, and you can see this in the way food often appears in everyday conversations.

'HAVE YOU EATEN BREAKFAST?'

This is a common expression, especially among parents and particularly for those with children living away from home. It's a heartfelt way for parents to express their genuine concern and care for their child's wellbeing; and their worry extends beyond just whether their children are eating, they're also deeply interested in how their children are navigating life. This phrase underlines the importance of a wholesome breakfast, for both physical and mental health.

'HI, HAVE YOU HAD LUNCH?'

You will often hear this in business meetings in Korea – it might seem a bit out of the ordinary compared to the typical 'How are you doing?', however, it's a warm and friendly way to convey a sincere concern for the other person's wellbeing and how their day has been unfolding.

'LET'S HAVE DINNER OUT.'

A customary way to arrange appointments, even if there's no intention to dine together, this phrase signifies the intention to maintain a connection and extend goodwill. 'Let's have dinner sometime,' is often used to bring conversations to a close, even between individuals who may not be particularly close or for whom future meetings are uncertain. It's a polite way to keep those connections alive and warm.

THE FIVE TRADITIONAL KOREAN COLOURS

Obangsaek, the classic five-colour spectrum in Korean culture, embodies harmony and balance. These colours represent cardinal directions and essential life elements: blue/green for east and wood; red for south and fiery energy; yellow for centre and soil; white for west and the strength of metal; and black for north and water. You can spot these colours in various aspects of Korean culture, from *hanbok* (traditional attire) to paintings, architecture, flags, and traditional symbols.

They also play a role in Korean cuisine, where ingredients in harmony with these colours are believed to connect individuals to the universe's energy, carrying philosophical meanings.

Bibimbap (see page 51) is a prime example of this. Known for its diverse ingredients which create a harmonious flavour profile, this beloved Korean dish reflects the essence of *obangsaek* and can be seen on the cover artwork, below.

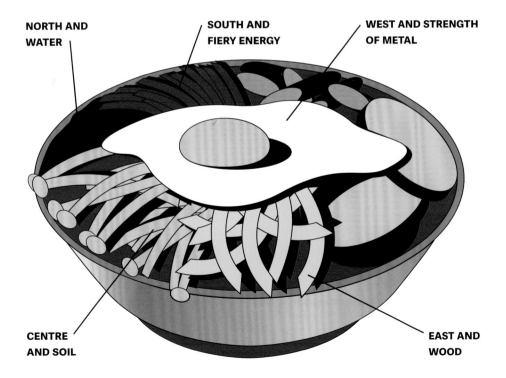

NORTH AND WATER

SOUTH AND FIERY ENERGY

WEST AND STRENGTH OF METAL

CENTRE AND SOIL

EAST AND WOOD

SEVEN KEY INGREDIENTS IN KOREAN COOKING

Korean cuisine is renowned for its bold flavours. There are seven essential ingredients that make it exceptional: gochujang, doenjang, gochugaru, ganjang (soy sauce), aekjeot (fish sauce), sesame oil and short-grain rice. I suggest you buy traditional Korean products – they really make a difference. Here is a quick summary of each one.

GOCHUJANG
(FERMENTED CHILLI PASTE)

There are many hot sauces in the world but, in my opinion, nothing compares with gochujang. Made with fermented soybeans and chilli, it's a full-flavoured, umami-rich paste with sweet and spicy notes – perfect for soups, stews, stir-fries, barbecue sauces and marinades.

DOENJANG
(FERMENTED SOYBEAN PASTE)

This rich and savoury paste is made with soybeans, salt and a fermentation starter called *meju*. Comparable to Japanese miso but far deeper in flavour, doenjang is full of funky, salty flavours. It works as a base for stews, salad dressings and glazes.

GOCHUGARU *(KOREAN RED CHILLI POWDER)*

Known for its bold and complex flavours, gochugaru is a common ingredient in various spice blends and seasonings.

There are two main types, coarse and fine, and each has its own unique properties and uses, making them essential components in traditional Korean dishes.

Coarse gochugaru is made from larger chillies that are typically sun-dried then ground to a coarse powder. It has a distinctive texture and a deep red colour and is commonly used in recipes that require a more substantial and robust spicy flavour, such as Kimchi (see page 21) and Kimchi Stew with Pork (see page 84).

Fine gochugaru is smoother in texture and lighter in colour. It is often used in recipes that require a milder chilli flavour, such as Oven-baked Kimchi Pancakes (see page 142), Korean Fried Chicken (see page 106) and pickled vegetables. It is also a common ingredient in Korean marinades and dipping sauces.

I recommend you use the two types separately to control the texture and colour of the final dish, but they can also be mixed.

GANJANG *(KOREAN SOY SAUCE)*

You may already have soy sauce in your cupboard,
but Korean soy sauce has its own subtle and distinct
taste. Lighter in colour than other varieties, salty and
a little sweet, it plays a key role in Korean-style
Barbecue Beef (see page 93), and other stir-fried or
braised dishes. I suggest choosing a naturally
brewed, all-purpose ganjang for the recipes in this
book; you can also use tamari for a gluten-free
option.

AEKJEOT *(KOREAN FISH SAUCE)*

This pungent, salty condiment is made
from fermented fish and its umami-rich
flavour enhances many dishes, from
stir-fries to marinades; it is also an
essential ingredient of kimchi. Authentic
Korean fish sauce can be difficult to find
outside of Korea so, an alternative, I
recommend Three Crabs Fish Sauce,
available at most Asian stores, or online.
Soy sauce or vegan fish sauce (usually
made from seaweed) are fish-free options,
but don't have the same intensity.

SESAME OIL

Sesame oil does a lot of heavy lifting in the Korean kitchen. It's made by pressing roasted sesame seeds and has a rich, nutty aroma that complements many dishes, including Korean-style Barbecue Beef (see page 93) and Glass Noodle Stir-fry (see page 62). Go for pure, roasted sesame oil as the taste of blended versions simply can't compete.

SHORT-GRAIN RICE

Koreans take great comfort in a simple bowl of steaming white rice. Korean short-grain rice is a high-quality variety that has been cultivated for thousands of years. It is usually cooked in a rice cooker and is fluffy when the grains are separate, and sticky when they clump, with a slightly sweet, nutty flavour that perfectly complements a variety of Korean dishes.

ADDITIONAL INGREDIENTS & ALTERNATIVES

Here are some other ingredients you might want to grab if you're planning to cook Korean food. While some can be found in supermarkets, most, if not all, of these are readily available at Asian grocery stores or can be found online. With these items in your pantry, you'll be well on your way to whipping up some delicious Korean dishes in no time.

SESAME SEEDS & BLACK PEPPER

When it comes to these two, there's one rule I have to stick to: it must be from Korea! While this isn't absolutely essential if you're just starting out on your Korean cooking journey, do be sure to use toasted sesame seeds and finely ground black pepper – your final dishes just won't taste the same without them!

NOODLES

Korean cuisine offers a wide variety of noodle options, from chewy sweet potato 'glass' noodles – or dangmyeon – used in the Glass Noodle Stir-fry known as japchae (see page 62), to thin wheat noodles called somyeon, perfect for lighter broth-based dishes. Dangmyeon may be replaced with Chinese wide glass noodles (made with sweet potato) or Vietnamese vermicelli (made with rice). Wheat-based Italian vermicelli could also be used as a substitute for soup or sauce dishes that require somyeon.

TTEOKBOKKI TTEOK

This name refers to the cylindrical- or oval-shaped rice cakes used in the popular Korean dish tteokbokki (see pages 113 and 121). They are made from rice flour and have a chewy, slightly sticky texture.

TOFU

Stock up on both firm and silken varieties. Silken tofu is best for soups, while firm tofu is essential for stir-frying recipes.

KELP

Also known as kombu, this seaweed is an essential ingredient in kimchi fermentation and the base for various savoury soup creations. If you're short on time, ready-made seafood stock can be a convenient substitute in soups.

GIM

Some Koreans have a preference for referring to dried seaweed sheets – widely used in Korean dishes – as gim rather than nori. This was traditionally a way to reclaim and emphasize Korea's language and cultural identity after the period of Japanese colonialism. Gim comes in two forms: snack-sized, seasoned rectangles and larger unseasoned sheets. Gim seasoned with sesame oil and salt is a popular snack, while the larger sheets are perfect for making Korean Seaweed Rice Rolls , known as gimbap (see page 115). They are often thinner and boast a richer sea flavour than the nori typically used for sushi, although if you really can't find gim, then nori can be used as a substitute.

RAMYEON

Korean ramyeon and Japanese ramen are both noodles but with distinct differences. Ramyeon is a dried, instant packet noodle, while ramen is typically made fresh. Korean ramyeon is bold and spicy and often made with a savoury broth based on beef, chicken or seafood, whereas Japanese ramen offers various milder flavours like soy sauce, miso and a pork bone broth. Korean noodles are also thicker and chewier, which complements the strong flavours. Keep packet ramyeon on hand for quick and easy meal options. Don't be afraid to get creative with your instant noodles – see page 126 for my favourite hacks to make ramyeon even more enjoyable.

SOJU

Korea's national drink is the perfect choice for any gathering or celebration, infusing it with a touch of tradition and uniqueness. This spirit is usually based on a blend of rice and other grains and is often referred to as Korean vodka. Soju is a versatile base for drinks and can be a substitute for vodka in most cocktails (see pages 165–167).

SPRING ONIONS & GARLIC

Both staples in Korean cooking, spring onions (scallions) and garlic bring a natural umami flavour to dishes.

KOREAN RADISHES

With their firm and crunchy texture and peppery flavour, white Korean radishes are particularly favoured for Korean food and making kimchi. If you can't get Korean radishes then daikon (also known as mooli) can be used as an alternative.

한식

THE CLASSIC
KOREAN TABLE

In Korea, an everyday meal is a celebration of flavours, textures and, often, communal dining. This is reflected in the classic Korean table, which typically contains *banchan*, a collection of small side plates, served alongside the main soup and a warm bowl of The Perfect Steamed Rice (see page 48), and/or Korean barbecue.

Koreans also often turn to noodles as an alternative to traditional rice-based meals, while kimchi, a spicy and tangy fermented vegetable dish, adds an extra kick.

KIMCHI & PICKLES

1

Kimchi is made by pickling and fermenting vegetables. It has gained worldwide popularity in recent years, thanks to its unique taste and various health benefits. With more than 100 different versions, each with its own regional characteristics and family recipes, kimchi is Korea's national dish.

While kimchi is now readily available in restaurants and stores, I would like to share some super-easy recipes to make your own kimchi and pickles. We'll start with the Easy Classic Kimchi (see page 21), before exploring others, such as Tangy Cucumber Pickle (see page 26), a Vegan White Kimchi (see page 23) and Coriander Kimchi Salad (see page 27).

MY MOTHER'S LOVE FOR KIMCHI:
A SYMBOL OF AFFECTION

Kimchi, a fermented vegetable dish, is an essential part of any Korean meal. It holds a special place in every Korean's heart, and is more than just food. For me, it represents the love and care of my mother, and I cherish it dearly. Despite the physical distance between us, our bond remains strong.

Whenever my mother visits me from Korea, her first priority is to shop for kimchi ingredients. She prepares a variety for me, including the classic version, pickled radish cubes and pickled vegetables. Even after she leaves, my mother worries about me and ensures that I can still enjoy her kimchi by teaching me how to preserve it. For her, kimchi is not just food; it is a gift, an act of kindness for her daughter, a symbol of affection.

☺ SEJI'S TIPS

- Fish sauce and kelp are key players in the making of kimchi, providing deep and bold flavours. Soy sauce is a suitable vegan substitute for the fish sauce.
- If you don't have glutinous rice flour, then plain (all-purpose) flour can be used (rather than non-glutinous rice flour), despite slight textural differences. The flour helps the seasoning sauce adhere better to the cabbage, ensuring a well-coated, flavourful final product.

막김치

EASY CLASSIC KIMCHI

MAK KIMCHI

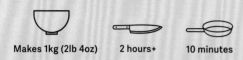

Makes 1kg (2lb 4oz)   2 hours+   10 minutes

INGREDIENTS

1kg (2lb 4oz) Chinese cabbage,
 trimmed
300g (10½oz) coarse salt
1 litre (1¾ pints) water
150g (5½oz) Korean radish (or daikon/
 mooli), cut into thin strips
100g (3½oz) spring onions (scallions),
 roughly chopped

For the rice slurry
1 tablespoon glutinous rice flour or
 plain (all-purpose) flour
250ml (9fl oz) water

For the kimchi paste
5 large garlic cloves, minced
10g (¼oz) fresh root ginger, minced
200g (7oz) Korean pear, peeled and
 minced (or 200ml/7fl oz apple juice)
1 tablespoon sugar
80g (2¾oz) coarse gochugaru
5 tablespoons fish sauce

Making kimchi is a simple three-step process: Brine – Season – Ferment. Over time, the saltiness will soften and the fermented vegetables will taste sour and complex. I like my kimchi strong, sour and zingy, so I ferment my vegetables for longer.

Step 1: Brine
1. Cut the Chinese cabbage into bite-sized (about 3cm/1¼in) squares. Dissolve the salt in the measured water in a large bowl. Soak the cabbage in this brine at room temperature for about 1 hour – turning occasionally to ensure it is fully brined. Once the soaking process is complete, the cabbage will become flexible. Rinse the leaves in running water and squeeze out excess water.

Step 2: Season
1. To make the rice slurry, dissolve the rice flour in the measured water in a pan and boil it over a medium-low heat until it thickens. Keep stirring to ensure no lumps form. Leave to cool to room temperature.

2. In another large bowl, combine the rice slurry and all the kimchi paste ingredients and mix through.

3. Add the brined cabbage to the bowl. Mix everything well by hand (use disposable gloves if you can) until all the pieces are well coated with the kimchi paste.

Step 3: Ferment
1. Transfer the kimchi to an airtight container or a sterilized jar, leaving space for expansion (3–5cm/1–2in) when it starts fermenting. Leave at room temperature for a day (2 days in winter). Then move to the refrigerator, it's ready to eat after 4–5 days and will last for 1 month.

깍두기

CUBED PICKLED RADISH

KKAKDUGI

The radish provides a refreshing crunch and a slightly sweet taste that complements the spicy, savoury flavour of the paste. The slower fermentation process here compared to other varieties of kimchi ensures a strong taste – this makes a perfect topping for rice bowls and salads or filling for sandwiches.

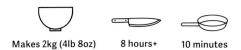

Makes 2kg (4lb 8oz)   8 hours+   10 minutes

INGREDIENTS
2kg (4lb 8oz) Korean radish (or daikon/mooli), peeled
2 tablespoons coarse salt
5 spring onions (scallions), sliced

For the rice slurry
1 tablespoon glutinous rice flour (or all-purpose flour)
250ml (9fl oz) water

For the kimchi paste
6 tablespoons coarse gochugaru
½ onion, reduced to a pulp in a blender
3 tablespoons fish sauce
3 tablespoons minced garlic
½ tablespoon minced fresh root ginger
2 tablespoons sugar

Step 1: Brine
1. Cut the radish into 3cm (1in) cubes. Put the cubed radish into a large bowl. Add the salt and mix well. Leave to brine for at least 7–9 hours or overnight.

2. Once the brining process has finished, drain the radishes out of the salt: don't rinse them with water.

Step 2: Season
1. To make the rice slurry, dissolve the rice flour in the measured water in a pan and boil it over a medium-low heat until it thickens. Keep stirring to ensure no lumps form. Remove from the heat and leave to cool to room temperature.

2. Put the cooled rice slurry and all the kimchi paste ingredients in a large bowl and mix well.

Step 3: Ferment
1. Add the radish and spring onions to the bowl of kimchi paste, and mix, making sure everything is evenly coated. Add to a sterilized glass jar, leaving a space at the top to allow for fermentation gases.

2. Leave at room temperature for a day, then put the kimchi in the refrigerator to slow down fermentation. Don't skip this process as it gives the kimchi its flavour. Eat after 1 week, store for up to 10 weeks.

백김치

VEGAN WHITE KIMCHI

BAEK KIMCHI

Makes 1kg (2lb 4oz)   2 hours+   10 minutes

Koreans began using red chilli pepper in the seventeenth century. One of its forms is gochugaru, a key ingredient in red kimchi. Until that time, white kimchi was the traditional style. Today, white kimchi is still a fresh and healthy alternative to red kimchi. It has a low sodium content that has a clean taste, with a soft texture that makes it perfect for toppings and salads. Its refreshing taste and health benefits make it a must-try for all kimchi lovers.

INGREDIENTS

1kg (2lb 4oz) Chinese cabbage, trimmed
300g (10½oz) coarse salt, plus 2 tablespoons to season
1 litre (1¾ pints) water
600g (1lb 5oz) Korean radish (or daikon/mooli), thinly sliced
½ Korean pear, peeled and thinly sliced (optional)
½ apple, peeled and thinly sliced
200g (7oz) Asian chives or wild garlic, sliced into 5cm (2in) lengths (optional)
½ garlic clove, thinly sliced
20g (¾oz) fresh root ginger, thinly sliced
200g (7oz) red or yellow (bell) peppers, thinly sliced

For the kelp broth (dashi)

1 litre (1¾ pints) water
1 x 10cm (4in) square sheet of kelp

For the rice slurry

1 tablespoon glutinous rice flour or plain (all-purpose) flour
250ml (9fl oz) water

Step 1: Brine

1. Brine the cabbage following the method on page 21, but slice in half instead of bite-sized pieces.

Step 2: Season

1. Make the kelp broth (dashi) by pouring the measured water into a pan, adding the kelp and bringing to the boil. Remove the kelp and leave the broth to cool to room temperature.

2. To make the rice slurry, dissolve the rice flour in the measured water in a pan and boil it over a medium-low heat until it thickens. Keep stirring to ensure no lumps form. Remove from the heat and leave to cool to room temperature.

3. Mix the 2 tablespoons of salt, the kelp broth and the rice slurry in a bowl.

Step 3: Ferment

1. Add the remaining ingredients in a sterilized glass jar. Pour in the seasoning mixture and mix well, ensuring everything is evenly coated, leaving a space at the top of the jar to allow for fermentation gases.

2. Leave at room temperature for a day or two, then transfer to the refrigerator.

EASY CLASSIC KIMCHI

VEGAN WHITE KIMCHI

CUBED PICKLED RADISH

오이절임

TANGY CUCUMBER PICKLE

OI MUCHIM

Serves 4-6   20 minutes

A refreshing combination of crisp mini cucumbers, fiery chilli peppers and savoury pickling ingredients, this dish makes a great accompaniment to meals.

INGREDIENTS
6–8 mini cucumbers
1 green chilli pepper, chopped
1 red chilli pepper, chopped
60g (2¼oz) red onion, chopped

For the brine
1.5 litres (3¼ pints) water
2 tablespoons salt

For the pickle
400ml (14fl oz) water
240ml (8½fl oz) soy sauce
230ml (8¼fl oz) rice vinegar
200g (7oz) sugar
1 x 10cm (4in) sheet of kelp (optional)

1. Take one cucumber and place it between two chopsticks. Make thin diagonal slices on the top, then flip it and make the same cuts on the other side. Repeat this process for the remaining cucumbers.

2. For the brine, put the measured water and salt in a large bowl. Add the sliced cucumbers and let them soak for 15 minutes and a maximum of 20 minutes.

3. In a separate bowl, combine all the pickle ingredients and stir until the sugar dissolves.

4. Place the brined cucumbers, chopped chillies and onion in a container or jar. Pour the pickle mixture over them and let them marinate at room temperature for 30 minutes.

5. To serve, cut the pickled cucumbers into bite-sized pieces and arrange on a dish.

오이절임

CORIANDER KIMCHI SALAD

GOSU KIMCHI

Serves 2   5 minutes

INGREDIENTS
70g (2½oz) coriander (cilantro),
  roughly torn in half
½ white onion, thinly sliced
½ carrot, thinly sliced or julienned
1 tablespoon sesame oil
1 teaspoon toasted sesame seeds,
  crushed

For the kimchi dressing
1½ tablespoons soy sauce
1 tablespoon fish sauce
1 tablespoon lemon juice
1 tablespoon sugar
1 tablespoon orange marmalade (or
  any citrus fruit one)
1 tablespoon coarse gochugaru
½ spring onion (scallion), finely
  chopped
½ tablespoon minced garlic

Coriander (cilantro) is not your usual ingredient for kimchi but I have found that this recipe – my own, and one dear to my heart – works very well with Korean food. This salad is perfect for coriander-lovers and can be served as a fresh side dish with a main course such as Korean-style Barbecue Beef (see page 93).

1. Mix all the dressing ingredients in a large bowl until well combined.

2. Add the coriander (cilantro), onion, carrot, and sesame oil to the bowl and gently toss until the vegetables are evenly coated with the dressing.

3. Sprinkle crushed sesame seeds over the top of the salad. Serve immediately as a fresh and zesty side dish.

☺ SEJI'S TIP
You can make different versions of this recipe by substituting the coriander with basil or cabbage.

BELOW, TANGY CUCUMBER PICKLE, PAGE 26

ABOVE, CORIANDER KIMCHI SALAD, PAGE 27

토마토 김치

FRESH TOMATO KIMCHI

Serves 3–4   5 minutes

A fresh twist on traditional kimchi, this recipe combines the sweet and sour flavours of tomatoes with a generous dose of kimchi seasoning. Although the combination may seem unusual at first, one taste of it will reveal the perfect balance it offers. Prepare this simple recipe when you're in the mood for a lighter, unfermented version of kimchi.

INGREDIENTS
5–6 tomatoes
50g (1¾oz) chives, cut into 3–4cm
 (1¼–1½in) lengths
½ onion, thinly sliced
¼ yellow sweet (bell) pepper, thinly
 sliced

For the kimchi seasoning
4 tablespoons coarse gochugaru
1 tablespoon sesame oil
2 tablespoons soy sauce
1 tablespoon minced garlic
½ tablespoon minced fresh root
 ginger
2 tablespoons sugar
2 tablespoons lemon juice

1. Make a deep cross-shaped cut on the top end of each tomato, leaving only about 2cm (¾in) at the base intact.

2. Put the kimchi seasoning ingredients in a bowl and mix well together. Add the chives, onion and yellow (bell) pepper.

3. Gently stuff the tomatoes with the kimchi seasoning paste. Be careful not to tear the tomatoes apart.

4. Serve fresh or store in an airtight container in the refrigerator for 1–2 days.

SIDE DISHES

반찬

Also known as *banchan*, these petite dishes are served with everyday meals. Back in the day, after Sunday church service, my family went to the local market for groceries to find a variety of ingredients, whatever was in season. Then operation 'food prep' for the week ahead commenced.

My father, little brother and I dutifully followed my mother's instructions, meticulously preparing everything so Mum could make different *banchan*: Sautéed Cucumber (see page 35), Mashed Tofu & Broccoli (see page 38), Stir-fried Shredded Potatoes (see page 40), and Egg-mari (see page 42). All nestled within their own containers in the fridge. Making a big batch ensured we had food ready to roll all week. No fuss, no stress, just good eating alongside a bowl of rice – the Korean way.

묵은지볶음

STIR-FRIED AGED KIMCHI

MUGEUNJI BOKKEUM

Serves 3–4   5 minutes   15 minutes

INGREDIENTS

400g (14oz) aged kimchi, cut into
  bite-sized pieces
2 tablespoons sesame oil
1 tablespoon vegetable oil
1 spring onion (scallion), finely
  chopped
½ tablespoon minced garlic
½ tablespoon sugar
½ tablespoon fish sauce
250ml (9fl oz) water
Toasted sesame seeds, to garnish

If you have some aged kimchi at home, you can try making this delicious side dish with sesame oil. It is perfect for repurposing kimchi that has become sour and floppy due to over-fermentation, and can be served as a side dish or used as a filling in Korean Seaweed Rice Rolls, also known as gimbap (see page 114), or Cabbage Leaf Wraps with Tuna Ssamjang (see page 110).

1. Put the kimchi in a colander (strainer), and rinse with cold water. Shake off the excess and drain.

2. Heat the sesame oil and vegetable oil in a pan over a medium-low heat. Stir-fry the spring onion (scallion) and minced garlic until fragrant, then add the drained kimchi, sugar, and fish sauce. Stir-fry for a few more minutes.

3. Pour the measured water into the pan, cover with a lid, and braise over a medium-low heat for about 10–15 minutes.

4. Garnish with sesame seeds and serve hot or cold as a delicious side dish.

오이나물

SAUTÉED CUCUMBER

OI NAMUL

Serves 2 | 5 minutes plus salting | 5 minutes

This simple stir-fried cucumber covered with nutty sesame seeds is a perfect summertime dish and works well as a salad, but also as a topping for summer noodles or bibimbap.

INGREDIENTS
2 medium cucumbers, thinly sliced
1 teaspoon salt
1 tablespoon vegetable oil
1 red chilli pepper (optional), sliced
1 spring onion (scallion), finely
 chopped
1 tablespoon toasted sesame seeds
2 tablespoons toasted sesame oil

1. Put the sliced cucumbers and salt into a mixing bowl. Toss to coat evenly and set aside for about 20 minutes, then drain and squeeze the water out from the salted cucumbers.

2. Add the oil to a frying pan and quickly stir-fry the cucumber over a medium-high heat until slightly cooked.

3. Add the chilli (if using) and spring onion (scallion), then stir-fry for a further 30 seconds. Remove from the heat, sprinkle with sesame seeds and drizzle with sesame oil.

고추된장무침

SOYBEAN GREEN CHILLI PEPPERS

GOCHU DOENJANG MUCHIM

Serves 3–4 | 5 minute

This dish works perfectly as an accompaniment to grilled meats.

INGREDIENTS
8–10 small mild peppers, such as
 Turkish chilli or mini (bell) peppers,
 cut into bite-sized pieces
2 spring onions (scallions), finely
 chopped
½ shallot, sliced

For the sauce
2½ tablespoons doenjang
1 tablespoon sesame seeds
1½ tablespoons sesame oil
2 tablespoons rice vinegar
2 tablespoons honey
2 tablespoons minced garlic
½ tablespoon soy sauce

1. Combine the sauce ingredients in a large bowl. Add more doenjang if you prefer.

2. Add the peppers, spring onions (scallions) and shallot, then toss them together so that the flavours mingle.

3. Transfer to a serving dish. Store any leftovers in the refrigerator: covered, they will stay fresh for 3–5 days.

1.

2.

3.

6.

7.

8.

4.

5.

9.

브로콜리 두부무침

MASHED TOFU & BROCCOLI

DUBU MUCHIM

Serves 2-3   5 minutes   3 minutes

A veggie-friendly side dish that tastes best straight from the refrigerator, where it can be stored for 2–3 days.

INGREDIENTS

1 head of broccoli, florets cut into
  bite-sized pieces
150g (5½oz) firm tofu
1 tablespoon soy sauce
1 teaspoon minced garlic
Sesame oil
Toasted sesame seeds
Salt to taste

1. Bring a pan of slightly salted water to the boil and blanch the broccoli florets for about 20 seconds. Lift them with a slotted spoon, rinse in cold water and drain.

2. Boil the tofu in the same pan of water for about 2–3 minutes. Drain and pat dry.

3. Roughly mash the tofu in a large bowl and add the broccoli. Combine it with the soy sauce, garlic, a drizzle of sesame oil. Sprinkle with sesame seeds and gently toss to coat evenly.

4. Transfer the tofu and broccoli mixture to a plate and finish it off with another generous sprinkle of sesame seeds.

계란찜

FLUFFY STEAMED EGG

GYERAN JJIM

Serves 2   5 minute   5 minutes

This dish is often provided free of charge at barbecue restaurants in Korea and is best served alongside rice.

INGREDIENTS

100ml (3½fl oz)   5 eggs, beaten
  water   1 spring onion
2 teaspoons fish   (scallion), sliced
  sauce   Sesame oil
1 teaspoon sugar   Toasted sesame
1 teaspoon salt   seeds
1 teaspoon
  sesame oil

1. Mix everything, except the spring onion, in a bowl. Pour the egg mixture into a small heavy-based pan with a lid, filling the pan to about 80%.

2. Put the pan over a medium heat, stirring constantly with a spatula to prevent the eggs from sticking to the bottom.

3. Reduce the heat to low, scatter the spring onion (scallion) over the egg, and cover with the lid. Steam for 3–5 minutes until the eggs are fully cooked and swelled up.

4. Carefully remove the lid and drizzle sesame oil over the eggs, then sprinkle with sesame seeds. Serve immediately.

SIDE DISHES

감자반찬

POTATO BANCHAN, TWO WAYS
STIR-FRIED SHREDDED POTATOES

GAMJA BOKKEUM

As in the West, potatoes are a staple in Korea, but while many Western potato dishes require deep frying or roasting, Korean ones focus on stir-frying and braising and can be served hot or cold.

BRAISED POTATOES

GAMJA JORIM

Serves 2 · 5 minutes · 5 minutes

Serves 2 · 5 minutes · 25 minutes

INGREDIENTS
Vegetable oil
1 spring onion (scallion), chopped
1 onion, sliced
½ carrot, sliced lengthways
2 medium potatoes, grated (shredded)
½ tablespoon salt
Toasted sesame seeds

1. Heat a little oil in a frying pan over a medium heat. Stir-fry the chopped spring onion.

2. Add the onion, carrot and potatoes and continue to stir-fry over a medium heat until the potatoes become transparent.

3. Turn off the heat and season with the salt.

4. Sprinkle with sesame seeds and serve!

INGREDIENTS
1kg (2lb 4oz) baby potatoes, washed but unpeeled
Toasted sesame seeds

For the sauce
350ml (12fl oz) water
4 tablespoons soy sauce
3 tablespoons rice syrup (or sugar)
1 tablespoon vegetable oil
½ tablespoon sesame oil

1. Boil the baby potatoes until fully cooked (about 20 minutes). Meanwhile, whisk together the ingredients for the sauce.

2. Drain the potatoes, return them to the pan and add the sauce. Stir over a medium-low heat.

3. Turn up the heat to medium. Keep stirring and cooking until the sauce is reduced and the potato skin is glossy and wrinkled.

4. Remove from the heat and sprinkle with sesame seeds.

5. Plate up and serve with a bowl of The Perfect Steamed Rice (see page 48).

꽈리고추찜

STEAMED PADRÓN PEPPERS

PADRÓN PEPPER JJIM

Serves 2

5 minutes

5 minutes

INGREDIENTS
150g (5½oz) padrón peppers
3 tablespoons plain (all-purpose)
 flour
½ tablespoon sesame oil
Toasted sesame seeds, to garnish

For the sauce
1 tablespoon coarse gochugaru
2 tablespoons soy sauce
1 tablespoon honey
½ tablespoon minced garlic
½ red chilli pepper, finely chopped
1 spring onion (scallion), finely
 chopped

This dish is traditionally made with a type of Korean pepper known as *kkwari* (also known as *shishito*), which shares similarities with padrón peppers. For my take on this vibrant dish, I have chosen to use padrón peppers for ease, while still maintaining the tradition of steaming the peppers and dressing them with soy sauce. Serve as a side or starter.

1. Begin by washing the padrón peppers and pierce each with a fork. While slightly wet, coat with the flour – it's simplest to put the flour in a plastic bag with the peppers and shake the bag until the peppers are thinly and evenly coated.

2. Bring some water to the boil in a saucepan. Once boiling, place the peppers in a steamer basket and steam with the lid on for about 5 minutes. Transfer the basket to a tray and leave the peppers to cool to ensure the flour coating stays on.

3. Meanwhile, mix the ingredients for the sauce in a large bowl. Once the peppers have cooled, mix them in the sauce and then drizzle over the sesame oil.

4. Transfer the peppers to a serving plate and finish with a generous sprinkle of sesame seeds.

☺ SEJI'S TIP
As an alternative to steaming, try stir-frying the flour-coated peppers instead, then toss with the sauce and sesame oil.

계란말이

EGG-MARI

GYERAN MARI

Serves 2   5 minutes   10 minutes

INGREDIENTS
5 large eggs
¼ teaspoon fine sea salt
Pinch of sugar
Pinch of ground black pepper
2 tablespoons finely chopped spring
  onion (scallion)
2 tablespoons finely chopped carrot
Vegetable oil

My mom is a master of Egg-mari. When I was young, it was one of my favourite *banchan* for school lunch. The egg roll may look difficult to achieve but it's actually very simple (and quick!) to cook.

1. Crack the eggs into a bowl and beat together. Stir in the salt, sugar and black pepper before mixing in the spring onion (scallion) and carrot.

2. Heat a frying pan over a medium-low heat and add some vegetable oil.

3. Pour in half the egg mixture in and swirl it evenly to cover the base of the pan.

4. Once the edges are cooked, reduce the heat to low, and start rolling the egg with your spatula.

5. Push the rolled egg over to the side of the pan. Add a little more oil if needed, and pour in more of the remaining egg mixture. Cook then roll as before. Repeat until all the egg mixture is used up.

6. Remove from the pan and let it cool down. Slice the egg roll into bite-sized slices and serve with ketchup.

고추장 달걀 조림

GOCHUJANG-BRAISED EGGS

GOCHUJANG GEARAN

Serves 3–4

5 minutes

15 minutes

INGREDIENTS
12 padrón peppers
10 eggs
½ onion, sliced
1 tablespoon finely chopped chives
1 teaspoon salt

For the sauce
250ml (9fl oz) water
2 tablespoons gochujang
1 tablespoon fine gochugaru
2 tablespoons soy sauce
1 tablespoon sugar
2 tablespoons honey
½ teaspoon ground black pepper
1 tablespoon fish sauce

To garnish
Sesame oil
Toasted sesame seeds
Chopped chives (optional)

This recipe puts a flavour-filled twist on the traditional method of simmering eggs in soy sauce. The combination of boiled eggs with padrón peppers bathed in a rich gochujang sauce makes a wonderful addition to any meal, either on its own or served as a side dish alongside rice.

1. Begin by washing the padrón peppers and making small holes in each one with a fork to allow the seasoning to penetrate. Set aside.

2. Pour enough water into a large pan to cover the eggs, add the salt and bring to the boil. Lower in the eggs and boil for 6–8 minutes for a hard-boiled texture with a slightly soft yolk. The salt makes shelling the eggs easier. Meanwhile, whisk all the sauce ingredients together in a bowl.

3. Drain and put the eggs in cold water to cool. Once cool, shell the eggs.

4. Pour the measured water into a fresh pan, add the remaining sauce ingredients and bring to the boil. Once the sauce starts to boil, add the eggs, onion, chives and peppers to the pan. Cook for about 5–8 minutes over a medium heat, stirring regularly, until the sauce reduces and thickens and the padrón peppers are wrinkled.

5. Transfer to a serving dish and drizzle with sesame oil. Sprinkle sesame seeds and chopped chives on top. Enjoy!

RICE & NOODLES

밥, 국수

3

At the heart of a classic Korean meal is rice, a staple that is consumed daily. It acts as a neutral, filling base to many dishes, such as the much-loved bibimbap, with its endless combinations: try the classic version of Rice & Vegetables with Beef on page 51, a Spicy Sushi Salad Bibimbap on page 54, or my Super-quick Egg Bibimbap (see page 49) is perfect for those in a rush.

Koreans often turn to noodles as an alternative to traditional rice-based meals; these strands of goodness hold symbolic meanings, representing longevity and love in life and marriage. From the beloved Glass Noodle Stir-fry, known as japchae (see page 62), to the rich and comforting broth of Kalguksu (see pages 67 and 68), Korean noodles offer a range of flavours and textures.

쌀밥

THE PERFECT STEAMED RICE

BAP

Serves 2-3   15 minutes   20 minutes

INGREDIENTS
200g (7oz) short-grain rice
200ml (7fl oz) water

A Korean meal is never complete without a bowl of shiny white rice, but it can be tricky for first-timers to cook it just right. Crucially, the amount of rice and water has to be in a 1:1 ratio. It's as simple as that. Now, let me walk you through the easy steps to achieve the perfect steamed rice, every time.

1. Gently rinse the rice until the water runs clear. Soak your rinsed rice in cold water for 10 minutes, allowing it to absorb moisture so it will cook more evenly.

2. Drain the soaked rice through a strainer and transfer it to a pan with the measured water. Bring to the boil, uncovered, over a medium heat.

3. Once the water starts to boil, stir the rice, reduce the heat to low and cover the pan with a lid. Cook the rice for 10 minutes.

4. After the cooking time, turn off the heat and leave the pan, still covered, for a further 10 minutes – don't be tempted to remove the lid. This crucial step allows the steam to work its magic, resulting in fluffy and tender rice.

5. Your perfectly steamed rice is now ready to be served. Enjoy alongside your favourite dishes.

☺ SEJI'S TIP
I'm a rice-cooker fan. While it's true that you can cook rice well in a pan, if you regularly make rice, I encourage you to consider investing in a rice cooker. It simplifies the process and brings so much convenience to your Korean cooking adventures.

계란밥

SUPER-QUICK EGG BIBIMBAP

GYERAN BAP

Serves 1   5 minutes   20 minutes

INGREDIENTS
½ batch The Perfect Steamed Rice
 (see opposite), warm
1 egg
Neutral oil, for frying
1 tablespoon soy sauce
½ tablespoon butter
Seasoned gim, crushed

A childhood staple for many, including myself, is the humble egg bibimbap, or gyeran bap. I have memories of my mother lovingly preparing this quick and comforting meal for me. I would wake from a nap to the aroma of savoury butter coating the warm rice. I loved it so much that I always asked for seconds!

This recipe is comforting and warm: a hug in a bowl. Let its simplicity and familiar flavours bring you contentment, just as it did for me throughout my childhood. Plus, when you're pushed for time, it's the perfect dish.

1. Start by preparing your rice, keep warm.

2. Fry the egg in a little oil, sunny side up. Place the egg on top of the warm rice.

3. Add the soy sauce and butter. Top it off with crushed gim. *Bibim* (mix) it! Enjoy!

☺ SEJI'S TIP
Everyone who makes this adds their own unique twist, and you can too – perhaps by substituting the fried egg for canned tuna, or adding a tablespoon of gochujang with butter instead soy sauce, you get the idea.

비빔밥

RICE & VEGETABLES WITH BEEF

BIBIMBAP

Serves 2   15 minutes   20 minutes

INGREDIENTS

1 batch The Perfect Steamed Rice
  (see page 48), warm
150g (5½oz) spinach
150g (5½oz) bean sprouts
100g (3½oz) carrots, cut into strips
100g (3½oz) courgettes (zucchini),
  cut into strips
100g (3½oz) mushrooms, sliced
Neutral oil, for frying
80g (2¾oz) cucumber, sliced
Salt to taste

For the beef

100g (3½oz) beef, any cut, thinly
  sliced
1 tablespoon soy sauce
1 tablespoon sugar
½ teaspoon ground black pepper

For the gochujang sauce

40g (1½oz) gochujang paste
2 teaspoons soy sauce
2 teaspoons sugar
½ teaspoon minced garlic
1 teaspoon lemon juice (optional)

To serve

2 eggs, fried
Sesame oil
Toasted sesame seeds

Bibimbap is an iconic Korean rice dish and contains perfectly cooked rice as its foundation, topped with an array of toppings and flavours, including vegetables, protein, sweet and spicy gochujang sauce and aromatic sesame oil.

1. Start by preparing your rice (see page 48).

2. While your rice is cooking, blanch the spinach and bean sprouts in boiling water. Drain as soon as they're wilted then plunge them into cold water. Squeeze out the excess water and season with salt.

3. One by one, stir-fry the carrots, courgettes (zucchini) and mushrooms in oil with a pinch of salt.

4. Marinate the beef with the soy sauce, sugar and black pepper, then stir-fry over high heat for 2–3 minutes.

5. Mix the ingredients for the gochujang sauce in a small bowl.

6. Scoop the warm rice into 2 bowls and add the prepared vegetables, including the cucumber, and beef. Top each bowl with a fried egg, a drizzle of gochujang sauce, a swirl of sesame oil and a sprinkling of sesame seeds. *Bibim* (mix) it and enjoy!

야채 비빔밥

RICE & ROASTED VEGETABLES

YACHAE BIBIMBAP

Serves 2

15 minutes

30 minutes

INGREDIENTS

1 batch The Perfect Steamed Rice
(see page 48)
200g (7oz) vegetables – any, but
I recommend kale, red onion or
courgette (zucchini)
150g (5½oz) mushrooms (any)
150g (5½oz) mixed colours of (bell)
peppers
Extra virgin olive oil, for drizzling
2 eggs
Salt and ground black pepper

For the gochujang sauce
40g (1½oz) gochujang
2 teaspoons soy sauce
2 teaspoons sugar
1 teaspoon minced garlic
Lemon juice (optional)

To garnish
Sesame oil
Toasted sesame seeds

The possibilities are endless with this bibimbap! It's a stress-free vegetarian dish that can be rustled up easily in a roasting tin. You can use any veg you have.

1. Start by preparing your rice (see page 48), keep warm.

2. Meanwhile, preheat the oven to 200°C fan/425°F/gas mark 7. Whisk together the ingredients for the gochujang sauce.

3. Chop the vegetables, including the peppers, into even-sized slices. Tip everything (except kale, if using) into a large mixing bowl together with the mushrooms. Drizzle with extra virgin olive oil and add salt and pepper to taste.

4. Toss the medley to coat evenly, then transfer to a large roasting tin and even it out.

5. Roast for 20 minutes, until slightly caramelized.

6. Remove the tin from the oven. Carefully crack each egg into the vegetables, keeping the yolk intact, and add the kale (if using). Return the tin to the oven and bake until the egg whites have settled – about 5–8 minutes.

7. Remove from the oven. Divide the roasted vegetables and egg evenly between the 2 bowls of rice. Top with a drizzle of gochujang sauce, a swirl of sesame oil and a sprinkling of sesame seeds. *Bibim* (mix) it and enjoy!

회덮밥

SPICY SUSHI SALAD BIBIMBAP

HOE-DEOPBAP

Serves 2   15 minutes   20 minutes

INGREDIENTS

1 batch The Perfect Steamed Rice
 (see page 48)
200g (7oz) sushi-grade salmon, tuna
 or sea bass
90g (3¼oz) lettuce and baby salad
 leaves
100g (3½oz) cucumber, thinly sliced
Seasoned gim, crushed, to garnish

For the gochujang vinaigrette

40g (1½oz) gochujang
2 teaspoons soy sauce
2 teaspoons rice vinegar
2 teaspoons sugar
1 teaspoon lemon juice
1 teaspoon sesame oil
½ teaspoon minced garlic
1 teaspoon toasted sesame seeds

I love serving up this deliciously acidic sushi salad – the tangy, spicy gochujang really brings out the taste of fresh fish. It's delicious any time of year, but it's particularly good for a summer lunch.

1. Start by preparing your rice (see page 48).

2. Meanwhile make the gochujang vinaigrette: simply mix all the ingredients together until the sugar is dissolved.

3. Cut your chosen fish into bite-sized cubes, thinly slice the lettuce and prepare the baby salad leaves.

4. Scoop the rice into 2 bowls, top with the sushi, salad and cucumber with a drizzle of vinaigrette. *Bibim* (mix) it and enjoy, garnished with the gim.

쇠고기 죽

COMFORTING BEEF PORRIDGE

SOEGOGI JOOK

 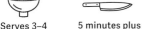

Serves 3–4 | 5 minutes plus marinating | 35 minutes

INGREDIENTS
500ml (18fl oz) water
360g (12½oz) The Perfect Steamed
 Rice (see page 48)
½ carrot, finely chopped
½ onion, finely chopped
Salt to taste

For the beef
300g (10½oz) minced (ground) beef
1 tablespoon soy sauce
1 tablespoon sesame oil
Pinch of ground black pepper

To garnish
Sesame oil
Toasted sesame seeds

This recipe of rice boiled in liquid until it has a thick, soupy texture is what we call *jook*. It's a nourishing, comforting Korean porridge which takes me right back to my grandma's kitchen. The traditional way is to make it from scratch using raw rice grains. However, my easy version uses leftover cooked rice. It's very simple, yet you won't forget how perfectly the meat juices and the soft, creamy rice blend together.

1. Marinate the beef in the soy sauce, sesame oil and black pepper. Set aside for 15 minutes.

2. Set a nonstick saucepan or pot over a low-medium heat, add the marinated beef and stir-fry for about 1–2 minutes.

3. Once the beef is cooked, pour the measured water into the pan, add the rice, carrot and onion and bring to the boil, uncovered.

4. Continue to boil over a medium heat for about 10–15 minutes. Gently stir to stop the rice from sticking to the bottom.

5. Reduce the heat to low, cover with a lid and simmer for a further 12–15 minutes or until the rice has a soft and creamy consistency. Taste and add salt and black pepper if needed.

6. Turn off the heat. Plate up and drizzle with 1 teaspoon of sesame oil per serving and sprinkle with sesame seeds. Serve hot.

☺ SEJI'S TIP
Instead of beef, you can also make this with the same weight of chicken, crab meat or mushrooms.

김치볶음밥

ONE-PAN KIMCHI-FRIED RICE WITH SPAM®

KIMCHI BOKKEUMBAP

Kimchi-fried rice and Spam® are two much-loved staples in Korean households, and it's easy to see why: this quick, filling and comforting dish comes together in just a few minutes. It's great way of using up ingredients. Leftover cooked rice and the sour taste of aged kimchi work perfectly for this.

Serves 2

5 minutes

5 minutes

INGREDIENTS

2 tablespoons vegetable oil, plus extra for the eggs
1 spring onion (scallion), plus extra to garnish, thinly sliced
80g (2¾oz) Spam®, cut into bite-sized cubes
150g (5½oz) kimchi, finely chopped
1 tablespoon sugar
½ tablespoon soy sauce
½ tablespoon fish sauce
1 batch The Perfect Steamed Rice (see page 48), at room-temperature
Sesame oil, for drizzling
2 eggs

1. Put the oil in a nonstick pan over medium-high heat and stir-fry the spring onion (scallion) and Spam® for 2 minutes.

2. Add the kimchi, sugar, soy sauce and fish sauce to the pan and stir-fry for a further 2 minutes. If the seasonings start to stick, add a dash of water.

3. Next, add your room-temperature rice and stir-fry over a high heat for 3 minutes.

4. Drizzle sesame oil over your ingredients and give them a good mix before removing the pan from the heat.

5. Heat a little extra oil in a small frying pan and fry the eggs. Add the eggs to the rice mix and finish with the extra sliced spring onion. Serve hot from the pan – just tuck in with a spoon.

☺ SEJI'S TIP
Why not try this recipe with beef, bacon, ham, or even chorizo in place of the Spam®?

김치죽

DAD'S KIMCHI RICE PORRIDGE

KIMCHI JOOK

Serves 1   5 minutes   25 minutes

INGREDIENTS
150g (5½oz) kimchi, cut into
   small pieces
3 tablespoons kimchi juice
2 tablespoons fine gochugaru
1 tablespoon soy sauce
½ tablespoon sesame oil
450ml (16fl oz) water
1 batch The Perfect Steamed Rice
   (see page 48)
½ tablespoon fish sauce
Salt to taste

To garnish
Finely chopped chives
Sesame oil

This is a bowl of pure nostalgia that takes me back to moments with my dad. Sometimes, when Mom's busy with her work, my dad steps in, armed with his fail-proof recipe for 'kimchi porridge'. This humble yet heart-warming dish, made with leftover rice and tangy kimchi, has become my go-to hangover meal and is a special reminder of my dad's love. The combination of perfectly cooked rice, infused with the vibrant flavours of sour kimchi, creates a comforting goodness that warms both body and soul.

1. Put the kimchi, kimchi juice, gochugaru, soy sauce and sesame oil in a pan over a medium-high heat and stir-fry for about 2 minutes.

2. Add the measured water and cooked rice to the pan and bring to the boil. Once boiling, reduce the heat to low.

3. Season with the fish sauce and salt, then simmer, uncovered, over a low heat, stirring occasionally, for 20–25 minutes or until the rice reaches the desired consistency. (I like my jook to have a thick and bold consistency but you can also have it on the soupy side.)

4. Scoop the porridge into a bowl and finish with chives and a swirl of sesame oil.

김치비빔국수

GRANDMA'S COLD SPICY NOODLES

KIMCHI BIBIM GUKSU

 Serves 2

 10 minutes

 10 minutes

This dish is a favourite for Koreans in the summertime. It is made with somyeon, thin wheat noodles enjoyed cold with a blend of sweet, spicy and savoury flavours from the gochujang and sour kimchi. This recipe has been passed down from my grandma – I haven't changed a thing! It is quick to prepare and stays true to its roots, preserving the love and care my grandma put into it.

INGREDIENTS
200g (7oz) kimchi, chopped
200g (7oz) somyeon (Korean thin wheat noodles)
1 hard-boiled egg, shelled and halved
½ cucumber, thinly sliced or julienned
Toasted sesame seeds

For the sauce
2 tablespoons gochujang
2 tablespoons white vinegar
1 tablespoon soy sauce
1 tablespoon kimchi juice
2 tablespoons sugar
1 tablespoon sesame oil

1. Put the chopped kimchi in a large bowl with all the sauce ingredients. Mix until well combined.

2. Cook the noodles in boiling water following the packet instructions. Once cooked, rinse the noodles under cold running water to remove the starch. Drain.

3. Place the cooked noodles in the bowl with the kimchi sauce and *bibim* (toss) until evenly coated.

4. Transfer the noodles to serving bowls and garnish with the egg, cucumber, and a sprinkle of sesame seeds. Enjoy!

☺ SEJI'S TIP
For an extra cool touch, serve the noodles over chilled ice cubes.

잡채

GLASS NOODLE STIR- FRY

JAPCHAE

Japchae is the ultimate party platter dish in my family. Its slightly sweet flavours and tender stir-fried ingredients are a real treat. Give it a go at your next gathering – just serve in a large dish so everyone can help themselves. It's a true crowd-pleaser!

Serves 4   10 minutes   15 minutes

R
I
C
E

&

N
O
O
D
L
E
S

INGREDIENTS
220g (7½oz) dangmyeon (sweet
  potato glass noodles)
120g (4½oz) baby leaf spinach
1 tablespoon vegetable oil
120g (4½oz) beef, any cut, cut into
  long strips
1 onion, thinly sliced
1 carrot, thinly sliced
200g (7oz) assorted mushrooms (I
  like shiitake), sliced
Drizzle of sesame oil
Toasted sesame seeds, to garnish
Salt and ground black pepper

For the dressing
8 tablespoons soy sauce
4 tablespoons sugar
8 tablespoons sesame oil
2 tablespoons minced garlic
2 tablespoons finely chopped spring
  onion (scallion)
½ tablespoon ground black pepper

1. Bring a large pan of water to the boil and cook the dangmyeon following the packet instructions until tender. Rinse in cold water and set aside.

2. Blanch the spinach in boiling water for about 10–15 seconds. Drain as soon as the leaves are wilted and plunge into cold water. Squeeze out the excess water and set aside.

3. Whisk all the ingredients for the dressing in a bowl.

4. Set a frying pan over a medium heat. Add the oil and stir-fry the beef with a pinch of salt. Once the beef is half cooked, after around 2 minutes, add the onion, carrot and mushrooms to the pan. Season with salt and pepper, then stir-fry for about 1–2 minutes.

5. Add the cooked noodles and spinach to the pan, along with half of the dressing. Drizzle sesame oil over the mixture and gently stir-fry for about 1–2 minutes; if the noodles are looking too dry, add some of the reserved dressing to taste.

6. To serve, transfer the noodles to a large platter, sprinkle sesame seeds over the top. Now it's time to celebrate!

☺ SEJI'S TIP
If you find your noodles are clumping together after rinsing with cold water, you can roughly cut the clumps with scissors to help separate them.

간장비빔국수

SOY SAUCE NOODLES

GANJANG BIBIM GUKSU

Serves 2

10 minutes

20 minutes

These moreish noodles are a firm favourite in my family – salty and sweet, they're light but addictive and very hard to stop eating. This recipe has been passed down from my grandma and I've adapted it to feature thin spaghetti noodles for an easy twist. I like to serve this with a raw egg yolk and a sprinkle of crushed gim (seasoned seaweed).

INGREDIENTS

200g (7oz) thin spaghetti or noodles (vermicelli, angel's hair or capellini work well)
20g (¾oz) finely chopped chives
2 egg yolks
Seasoned gim, crushed, to garnish

For the sauce

2 tablespoons soy sauce
2 tablespoons sugar
1 tablespoons sesame oil
½ garlic clove, minced
½ teaspoon ground black pepper
1 teaspoon toasted sesame seeds

1. Cook the noodles in a pan of boiling water following the packet instructions. Once cooked, rinse the noodles under cold running water to remove the starch, then drain.

2. Add the sauce ingredients to a large bowl and whisk to combine.

3. Add the cooked noodles to the bowl and *bibim* (toss) – I like to use my hands for this step to make sure the noodles are evenly coated.

4. Divide the dressed noodles between 2 plates, garnish with chopped chives and crushed gim and top each with an egg yolk.

짬뽕

SPICY SEAFOOD NOODLE SOUP

JJAMPPONG

Serves 1

5 minutes

15 minutes

This is an iconic Korean–Chinese dish that has captured the hearts and taste buds of many Koreans. It is typically served in Chinese restaurants and is a popular lunch choice for many Korean office workers.

Versions of this dish can be found in every corner of Korea, each with its unique take on the classic recipe. Typically made with a combination of fresh seafood and spicy soup, *jjamppong* is served with thick and chewy noodles that soak up the rich broth. Here is my easy version that uses spaghetti.

INGREDIENTS
2½ tablespoons vegetable oil
2 spring onions (scallions), sliced
1 tablespoon minced garlic
50g (1¾oz) minced (ground) pork or beef
½ onion, sliced
1–2 mushrooms, sliced
¼ courgette (zucchini), sliced
2 tablespoons coarse gochugaru
½ tablespoon soy sauce
550ml (1¼ pints) water
½ tablespoon chicken stock (bouillon) powder
½ tablespoon fish sauce
¼ tablespoon sugar
Pinch of ground black pepper
80g (2¾oz) spaghetti (you can also use vermicelli or udon noodles)

For the seafood mix
1–2 king prawns (jumbo shrimp), shell on
5–7 mussels, shell on
40g (1½oz) squid, cut into bite-sized pieces

1. Heat the oil in a large pan or wok over a medium heat. Add the spring onion (scallion), garlic and pork and stir-fry for 3 minutes until fragrant.

2. Add the onion, mushrooms, courgette (zucchini), gochugaru and soy sauce, and keep stir-frying.

3. Once the vegetables are halfway cooked, pour in the measured water then add the stock (bouillon), fish sauce, sugar and black pepper and stir to combine. Increase the heat to high and simmer the soup for 5 minutes to allow the flavours to meld.

4. Then, add all the seafood to the pot and simmer for a further 5 minutes until it is cooked through.

5. Meanwhile, cook the spaghetti according the packet instructions, then drain.

6. Put the spaghetti in a large bowl and ladle the soup on top. Serve immediately while piping hot. Slurping is allowed!

66

R
I
C
E

&

N
O
O
D
L
E
S

해물칼국수

KNIFE-CUT NOODLE SOUP WITH CLAMS

HAEMUL KALGUKSU

Serves 2-3 · 10 minutes plus soaking & resting time · 10 minutes

Kalguksu is a dish of simmering handmade noodles in a flavoursome broth. From the rustic allure of chicken-infused versions to the briny, coastal charm of seafood ones, each type captures the unique essence of its locale. This one uses a broth infused with dried kelp and clams, resulting in a rich, tasty, comforting dish.

INGREDIENTS
1.6 litres (3½ pints) water
4 x 10cm (4in) square sheets of kelp
  or 1 fish stock cube
1 tablespoon soy sauce
½ tablespoon fish sauce
1 medium potato, peeled and thinly
  sliced
300g (10½oz) handmade noodles (see
  below), or fresh tagliatelle
10–12 clams (or mussels), shell on
½ courgette (zucchini), sliced
½ tablespoon minced garlic
1 onion, sliced
2 spring onions (scallions), sliced
½ tablespoon salt (or more to taste)
Toasted sesame seeds, to garnish
Ground black pepper, to garnish

For the handmade noodles
350g (12oz) plain (all-purpose) flour,
  plus extra for dusting
150ml (5fl oz) water, at room
  temperature
1 tablespoon vegetable oil
1 teaspoon salt

1. For the broth, pour the measured water into a large bowl. Add the dried kelp and leave to soak for 15–20 minutes. Remove the kelp from the bowl and set aside.

2. Pour the kelp broth into a large pan. Add the soy and fish sauces and bring to the boil. Add the potatoes, noodles and clams to the boiling broth and cook for 5–7 minutes.

3. Now add the courgettes (zucchini), garlic, onions and spring onions (scallions), cook for 2–3 minutes, add the salt to taste, then remove the pan from the heat.

4. Divide between 2 bowls and sprinkle with sesame seeds and ground black pepper. Serve hot, with kimchi.

To make the handmade noodles
1. Thoroughly combine the ingredients in a large bowl. Knead the dough with your hands until it becomes smooth and elastic. Wrap in clingfilm and let it rest in the refrigerator for 30 minutes.

2. Dust the work surface with flour and use a rolling pin to roll out the dough to about 0.5cm (¼in) thick.

3. Fold the dough into thirds lengthways, dusting with flour as needed. Cut the dough into 0.5cm- (¼in-) thick pieces.

닭칼국수

MY SOUL-NOURISHING CHICKEN NOODLE SOUP

DAK KALGUKSU

Serves 2   5 minutes   35 minutes

This chicken noodle soup has been crafted in my own unique way, inspired by the flavours of North Korean cuisine. While the traditional method involves simmering a whole chicken with bones for a few hours to create a deep and rich broth, my easy version uses chicken breast seasoned with a spicy sauce to quickly prepare the soup base.

INGREDIENTS
2 litres (4¼ pints) water
200g (7oz) skinless chicken thigh fillets
2 onions, roughly chopped
6 garlic cloves, peeled
2 teaspoons salt
200g (7oz) fresh handmade noodles (see page 67) or fresh tagliatelle
½ small courgette (zucchini), cut into batons

For seasoning the chicken
1 tablespoon soy sauce
1 teaspoon ground black pepper
40g (1½oz) coarse gochugaru

To garnish
Spring onions (scallions), sliced

☺ SEJI'S TIP
To shred cooked chicken, place it on a board. Using two forks, anchor the meat with one fork and pull it apart with the other, shredding the chicken into your preferred size. Alternatively, you can shred it by hand.

1. Bring the measured water to the boil in a large pan. Add the chicken breast, onions, garlic and salt. Simmer for 20–25 minutes.

2. Once cooked, remove the chicken, onion and garlic from the broth using a slotted spoon. Allow the chicken breast to cool, then shred it. Mash the cooked garlic. Discard the cooked onion.

3. Combine the shredded chicken and mashed garlic in a bowl with the seasoning ingredients. Toss everything together.

4. Return the pan of chicken broth to a medium-high heat and bring it to the boil. Add the noodles and courgette (zucchini). Check for seasoning and add salt and black pepper to taste.

5. After 5–7 minutes, once the noodles are cooked, remove the pan from the heat.

6. Divide the noodles between 2 bowls. Top each bowl with the seasoned chicken and sprinkle with sliced spring onions (scallions). Serve piping hot.

SOUPS & STEWS

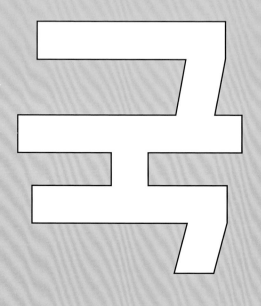

4

A key element of the everyday Korean meal, soups and stews are served in small individual bowls and intended to be eaten throughout the meal. They are often made with vegetables, meat or seafood simmered with fermented pastes to create a complex, flavour-filled broth.

While these types of dishes have a universal appeal, Koreans have a deep connection to these comforting creations, whether it's Korea's Official Hangover Soup (see page 76), a light bean sprout broth; Basic Soybean Paste Stew (see page 72), a popular umami-packed dish or Spicy 'Army Base' Stew (see page 83), a celebration of Eastern and Western flavours and ingredients.

된장찌개

BASIC SOYBEAN PASTE STEW

DOENJANG-JJIGAE

 Serves 2    5 minutes   10 minutes

This tasty and satisfying stew is Korean soul food. You can customize it to your liking, perhaps adding beef for a rich flavour or seafood for a salty kick; however, staying true to the basic recipe is a great option too. The stew features doenjang – savoury soybean paste – tofu and various vegetables. It's the perfect way to use up leftover veggies from your fridge and will leave you feeling comfortably full.

INGREDIENTS
480ml (17fl oz) water
1 medium potato, peeled and sliced into half moons
3 tablespoons doenjang
½ onion, sliced
¼ courgette (zucchini), sliced into half moons
1 tablespoon soy sauce
1 garlic clove, minced
1 spring onion (scallion), sliced
150g (5½oz) firm tofu, sliced
1 red chilli pepper, thinly sliced

1. Pour the measured water into a pan and bring to the boil. Add the potato and boil for 1 minute.

2. Add the doenjang, onion, courgette (zucchini) and garlic and boil for 5 minutes. Season with the soy sauce.

3. Add the spring onion (scallion) and tofu and boil for a further minute.

4. Serve hot with sides of rice and kimchi.

☺ SEJI'S TIP
Add more water for a lighter version, or, for a stronger flavour, increase the amount of doenjang and simmer for longer. I love gently mashing the tofu and eating this alongside warm rice.

계란오이국

CUCUMBER EGG DROP SOUP

GYERAN GUK

 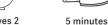

Serves 2   5 minutes   10 minutes

INGREDIENTS
800ml (1¾ pints) water
1 square sheet of kelp, or beef stock cube
½ tablespoon minced garlic
3 tablespoons fish sauce
150g (5½oz) cucumber, thinly sliced
1 small onion, sliced
1 red chilli pepper, sliced
3 eggs, beaten
½ teaspoon ground black pepper

To garnish
Spring onion (scallion), sliced

This soup is light and flavourful – the combination of cucumber and eggs creates a delicate balance of flavours that won't leave you feeling heavy.

1. Pour the measured water into a pan and add the kelp. Bring to the boil over a medium-high heat then simmer for 7 minutes.

2. Remove the kelp from the broth and increase the heat to high, then add the garlic, fish sauce, cucumber, onion and chilli pepper to the pan. Return to the boil.

3. Add the beaten eggs to the pan, stirring continuously to prevent the eggs from clumping. Keep boiling the soup until the eggs are fully cooked, for around 3–5 minutes.

4. Remove from the heat, divide between 2 bowls and sprinkle black pepper over the soup for an added flavour kick, as well as some sliced spring onion (scallion) to garnish.

☺ SEJI'S TIP
The soup is best enjoyed with a side of bread or rice and works well as a satisfying and refreshing breakfast or a light lunch.

콩나물국

KOREA'S OFFICIAL HANGOVER SOUP

KONGNAMUL GUK

Serves 2

5 minutes

30 minutes

This authentic bean sprout broth is light, refreshing and vitamin-packed – and a daily essential in Korea. It's also a very popular dish to make for breakfast after a night of drinking, as bean sprouts are thought to contain hangover-relieving compounds. I always keep some on standby in my refrigerator. Soybean sprouts are recommended, but other bean sprout varieties work well too. Say goodbye to hangovers, Korean-style!

INGREDIENTS
1.5 litres (3¼ pints) water
1 onion, roughly chopped
2 x 10cm (4in) square sheets of kelp,
 or 1 vegetable stock cube
1½ tablespoons soy sauce
150g (5½oz) bean sprouts, rinsed
1 spring onion (scallion), sliced
1 red chilli pepper, sliced
1 tablespoon minced garlic
Sea salt to taste
Seasoned gim, crushed, to garnish
 (optional)

1. Pour the measured water into a pan, add the onion and kelp and bring to the boil. Simmer for 20–25 minutes.

2. Remove the onion and kelp using a slotted spoon, then season the broth with the soy sauce and some sea salt. Continue to boil.

3. Add the bean sprouts, spring onion (scallion), chilli pepper and garlic to the broth. Simmer, uncovered, over a high heat for about 1 minute – no longer than 2 minutes.

4. Serve immediately in bowls, accompanied by a warm bowl of The Perfect Steamed Rice (see page 48). Garnish with crushed gim for an extra salty, umami kick.

꽃게된장찌개

DOENJANG CRAB SOUP

KKOTGETANG

Serves 2   5 minutes   10 minutes

INGREDIENTS

600ml (1¼ pints) water
20g (¾oz) doenjang
½ large potato, sliced into
 half-moons
½ onion, sliced
2 teaspoons coarse gochugaru
2 garlic cloves, minced
300g (10½oz) white crab meat
½ courgette (zucchini), sliced into
 half-moons
1 spring onion (scallion), sliced
Salt or fish sauce to taste

My grandma always cooked amazing dishes and her crab stew was my ultimate favourite. Her traditional version ideally uses fresh, live Korean crabs called *kkotge*, but for convenience I've simplified her recipe by using white crab meat. The doenjang adds depth and richness to the soup, while the crab meat lends a delicate sweetness.

1. Pour the measured water into a deep-sided pan and combine with the doenjang. Bring the mixture to the boil over a high heat.

2. Once boiling, add the potato, onion, gochugaru and garlic. Reduce the heat to medium and continue to boil for 5–7 minutes.

3. Add the crab meat, courgette (zucchini) and spring onion (scallion) to the broth. Boil for about 5 minutes. Taste and adjust the flavour by adding more doenjang, salt or fish sauce if you wish.

4. Transfer the broth to serving bowls and savour it alongside a warm bowl of The Perfect Steamed Rice (see page 48).

☺ SEJI'S TIP

If you're after a bolder seafood flavour, try adding around 150g (5½oz) of cod roe in Step 3, this will also bring a unique texture to the soup.

쇠고기무국

BEEF & RADISH SOUP

SOEGOGI MUGUK

Serves 3–4   5 minutes plus marinating   20 minutes

A much-loved traditional soup in Korean cuisine, this light and flavourful broth was a regular item on my family's menu and my mother used to make it with leftover radish after making kimchi. While soups and rice have traditionally been served separately in Korea, I enjoy having *gukbap*, which involves putting rice into the soup. This combination pairs perfectly with fresh kimchi.

INGREDIENTS

200g (7oz) beef brisket, cut into chunks
1.5–2 litres (3¼–4¼ pints) water
300g (10½oz) Korean radish (or daikon/mooli), cut into bite-sized pieces
½ onion, sliced
2–3 spring onions (scallions), sliced
½ tablespoon minced garlic
1 tablespoon soy sauce
1 tablespoon fish sauce
1 teaspoon salt
1 teaspoon ground black pepper

For the marinade

1 tablespoon soy sauce
½ tablespoon minced garlic
1 tablespoon sesame oil
½ teaspoon ground black pepper

1. Mix the beef and marinade ingredients in a bowl and leave to marinate for about 10 minutes.

2. Put a deep nonstick pan over a low heat and stir-fry the marinated beef for about 2 minutes. Pour in the measured water and add the radish. Increase the heat to high, bring to the boil, then reduce the heat to medium and simmer for 10–12 minutes until the radish is cooked.

3. Add the onion, spring onions (scallions), garlic, soy sauce and fish sauce to the pan and boil for a further 2 minutes. Season with the salt to maintain the clarity of the soup.

4. Sprinkle ground black pepper over the soup and serve it hot. Enjoy!

☺ SEJI'S TIP

You can also substitute in Chinese cabbage leaves, cut into bite-sized pieces, instead of the radish and cook for the same amount of time.

순두부 찌개

SPICY SILKEN TOFU SOUP WITH SEAFOOD

SUNDUBU JJIGAE

Serves 1

5 minutes plus soaking

10 minutes

S
O
U
P
S

&

S
T
E
W
S

INGREDIENTS
8–10 clams, shell on
2 tablespoons sesame oil
1 tablespoon vegetable oil
1 spring onion (scallion), sliced
½ small onion, sliced
2 tablespoons coarse gochugaru
1 tablespoon minced garlic
450ml (16fl oz) water
1 tablespoon soy sauce
1 tablespoon fish sauce
½ tablespoon sugar
1–2 king prawns (jumbo shrimp), shell
 on
300g (10½oz) silken tofu
1 egg yolk
Salt to taste

To garnish
Spring onion (scallion), sliced
Ground black pepper
Sesame oil

This silken tofu soup is one of the most popular dishes in Korean restaurants. It is a soothing dish that combines hot and spicy flavours with vegetables, protein and eggs.

1. Soak the clams in salted water for at least 20 minutes.

2. Meanwhile, heat the sesame oil and vegetable oil in a pan over a low-medium heat. Add the spring onion (scallion) and onion and fry until they start to sizzle.

3. Add the gochugaru and minced garlic. Stir well for about 1 minute. Be careful not to burn the garlic.

4. Pour in the measured water and increase the heat to medium-high. Once the soup starts to boil, add the soy sauce, fish sauce, sugar, clams and king prawns (jumbo shrimp).

5. When the clams start to open up, add the silken tofu and continue to boil for a further 2–3 minutes.

6. Drop the egg yolk into the soup and turn off the heat. Season with salt, if needed.

7. Top with spring onion, black pepper and a drizzle of sesame oil. Serve hot with a bowl of The Perfect Steamed Rice (see page 48). Enjoy!

☺ SEJI'S TIP
If you prefer a milder taste, you can substitute the clams for oysters and reduce the amount of gochugaru.

부대찌개

SPICY 'ARMY BASE' STEW

BUDAEJJIGAE

Serves 4 | 10 minutes | 5 minutes

INGREDIENTS

200g (7oz) Spam®, sliced into
  bite-sized pieces
60g (2¼oz) minced (ground) beef
2 spring onions (scallions), sliced
100g (3½oz) Frankfurter sausages,
  sliced
½ large onion, sliced
50g (1¾oz) aged kimchi, sliced into
  bite-sized pieces
30g (1oz) baked beans (Boston baked
  beans)
540ml (19fl oz) water
1 pack of ramyeon noodles, without
  flavour and vegetable packets
1 slice of American-style cheese
  (optional)

For the seasoning sauce
1 tablespoon minced garlic
2 tablespoons coarse gochugaru
1½ tablespoons gochujang
1 tablespoon soy sauce
1 teaspoon ground black pepper

☺ **SEJI'S TIP**
If you prefer your stew more soupy, add a little
more water at the end of Step 2.

This is a flavour-packed hotpot where savoury kimchi, indulgent Spam®, spicy gochujang, creamy cheese and hearty baked beans (Boston beans) come together in a mouth-watering fusion that represents the vibrant culinary melting-pot of Seoul. The origins of this dish are rooted in the use of surplus processed foods and canned goods at US military bases in Korea during the poverty period after the Korean War. Despite its humble beginnings, this stew has stood the test of time and continues to be a favourite for many Koreans.

It's my go-to dish to make for friends – prepared in a large pot and enjoyed as a communal meal, this is comforting food that brings people together, using inexpensive, easily accessible ingredients.

1. Whisk all the ingredients for the sauce together in a bowl. Put all the prepared ingredients in a large stockpot and add the sauce mixture.

2. Pour in the measured water and bring the stew to the boil over a high heat.

3. Once the stew starts boiling, add the instant ramyeon noodles. Boil for about 5 minutes over a high heat until the ramyeon is half cooked, then add a slice of American-style cheese on top of the ramyeon noodles, if using.

4. Once the noodles are cooked, serve the stew hot from the pot. This dish is already substantial with ramyeon providing a source of carbohydrates, but some people enjoy adding a bowl of rice to enhance the meal further.

김치찌개

KIMCHI STEW WITH PORK

KIMCHI JJIGAE

Kimchi stew is a much-loved Korean dish that can be made in many different variations. The tangy and spicy flavours of the kimchi cut the richness of the pork to create a unique and delicious taste that will leave you wanting more.

Serves 2

5 minutes

30 minutes

INGREDIENTS
500ml (18fl oz) water
130g (4½oz) pork shoulder or pork belly, sliced into bite-sized pieces
½ tablespoon fish sauce
360g (12½oz) sour kimchi, sliced into bite-sized pieces
2 garlic cloves, minced
2 tablespoons coarse gochugaru
1 spring onion (scallion), sliced, plus extra to garnish
2 green chilli peppers, sliced
1 tablespoon soy sauce

1. Pour the measured water into a pan and add the pork and fish sauce. Bring it to the boil over a medium-low heat. Cook for 15–20 minutes until the meat has softened.

2. If the water has decreased significantly while making the meat broth, add some more. Add the kimchi, garlic and gochugaru. Keep boiling for about 10–15 minutes over a medium-high heat.

3. Add the spring onion (scallion) and green chilli peppers. Season the stew with the soy sauce and continue boiling for a further 2–3 minutes.

4. To finish, sprinkle some sliced spring onion over the stew. Serve hot with a bowl of The Perfect Steamed Rice (see page 48) and *banchan* (Korean side dishes, see Chapter 2).

찜닭

KOREAN SOY SAUCE-BRAISED CHICKEN

JJIMDAK

Serves 3–4   5 minutes   35 minutes

Jjimdak is chicken braised with vegetables with the addition of brown sugar, soy sauce and sesame oil. My version includes padrón peppers which bring a mild spiciness to the dish.

INGREDIENTS

1kg (2lb 4oz) boneless chicken thighs, skin on, cut into bite-sized pieces
200ml (7fl oz) water
200g (7oz) potatoes, cut into bite-sized pieces
1 small carrot, thickly sliced
½ tablespoon crushed chilli flakes
30g (1oz) mushrooms, sliced
130g (4½oz) padrón peppers

For the sauce

140ml (4¾fl oz) soy sauce
70g (2½oz) brown sugar
200ml (7fl oz) water
1 teaspoon minced fresh root ginger
2 tablespoons minced garlic
4 spring onions (scallion), sliced
3 tablespoons sesame oil

To garnish

Toasted sesame seeds
1 red chilli pepper, sliced

1. Combine all the sauce ingredients in a bowl.

2. Put the chicken, sauce and the measured water in a flameproof heavy-based casserole. Bring it to the boil over a medium-high heat and let it cook for about 10 minutes.

3. Add the potatoes, carrots and chilli flakes to the pot. Cover and continue cooking for a further 15 minutes.

4. Stir in the mushrooms and padrón peppers. Reduce the heat to medium-low and simmer for a final 8 minutes, keeping the lid on, to allow the flavours to meld.

5. Garnish with sesame seeds and the sliced red chilli. Serve hot with a bowl of The Perfect Steamed Rice (see page 48).

KOREAN BBQ

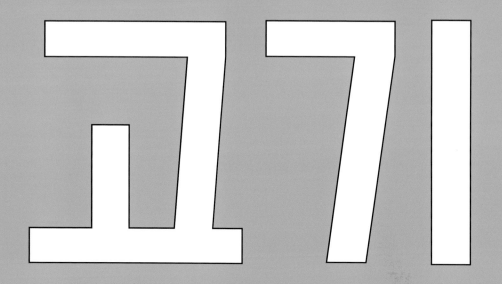

5

If you haven't tried Korean barbecue yet, you've been missing out on a truly unique dining experience. It's a feast for the senses – engaging, fun and, most importantly, the food is simply scrumptious. What sets Korean barbecue apart is that it's less about the method and more about its three essential elements: Marinate – Grill – Ssam!

This chapter contains recipes for whichever type of meat you prefer, such as Korean-style Barbecue Beef (see page 93), Spicy Stir-fried Pork (see page 99) or Spicy Stir-fried Chicken (see page 97). All the recipes can be cooked by the traditional indoor grill method (outlined on page 90), on an outdoor barbecue (see page 92), or conveniently in the kitchen on the hob or in the oven.

HOW TO INDOOR BARBECUE – KOREAN STYLE

STEP 1: MARINATE
Marinating the meat is where it all begins; whether it's a sweet and sticky soy sauce or a fiery gochujang mix, the flavours of Korean barbecue are rooted in the marinades that infuse the meat with umami goodness. Cutting the meat into thinner slices is essential, ensuring the seasoning and heat can permeate the meat evenly – the result is a truly authentic Korean flavour.

STEP 2: GRILL
Koreans traditionally gather with friends and family to grill delicious meat and veggies right at the dining table itself, using specific equipment, a method known as bulgogi. To recreate this communal dining experience at home, you can use a portable butane stove and a heavy-based frying pan, but just remember to keep the room properly ventilated by opening windows. Alternatively, you can use a heavy-based frying pan on the hob. And don't forget the essential tools for a Korean barbecue: tongs and cooking scissors. Cutting meat with scissors may be unfamiliar, but it's typical for Koreans and practical, too. For classic outdoor barbecue guidelines, see overleaf.

STEP 3: AND DON'T FORGET ABOUT SSAM!
One of the highlights of Korean barbecue is that you get to create your own wraps, known as ssam, using leafy greens and an assortment of ingredients. The wraps can be filled with a combination of meat, veggies and Ssamjang (see page 154). No matter what meat you choose to enjoy at a Korean barbecue, this one simple ingredient brings everything together. Literally meaning 'sauce for ssam', Ssamjang is a fermented soybean sauce that serves as the perfect dip for crunchy crudités, as well as a dressing for salads and ssam wraps.

HOW TO MAKE YOUR OWN SSAM

1. Lay a lettuce, chicory or perilla leaf (or both) in your hand.

2. Put a spoonful of rice in the middle.

3. Add meat, as well as other fillings of your choice, such as slices of chilli, kimchi, chives or other *banchan*. Traditionally, slivers of raw garlic are also addded.

4. Add a dollop of ssamjang on top.

5. Wrap the whole thing.

6. Eat it in one bite.

HOW TO OUTDOOR BARBECUE

STEP 1: PREPARE THE MEAT
Choose thinly sliced cuts of meat (you can find these at most Asian grocery stores) or slice the meat yourself, then marinate it according to the recipe. You can also prepare accompaniments such as kimchi and *banchan*, to be grilled alongside your meat for an authentic Korean touch.

STEP 2: PREPARE THE BARBECUE
Start by lighting the charcoal and letting it burn until it turns into white ash, then spread the coals evenly across the bottom of the grill. To prevent the meat from sticking, I recommend brushing the grill grate with oil; for thinly cut meat, I suggest using a thick grill grate to achieve the best results.

STEP 3: GRILL THE MEAT
Place the marinated meat on the hot grill, making sure not to overcrowd the surface. Begin by charring the meat on one side in the hottest heat zone of the grill for 2–3 minutes, allowing it to develop a nice sear or caramelization. Then flip the meat using tongs and char the other side for an additional 3–4 minutes until it's cooked through but still tender and juicy.

Remember, thinly sliced meat cooks quickly over a hot grill, so it's important to keep a close eye on the cooking time. In just minutes, you'll achieve that perfect balance of tender and juicy meat with a caramelized exterior.

STEP 4: SERVE AND ENJOY
Once the meat is cooked to their liking, diners can transfer it to a platter or individual plates. To elevate the experience, I encourage everyone to create ssam (wraps) with a dollop of some Ssamjang (see page 154). Instructions for making your own ssam are on page 90.

불고기

KOREAN-STYLE BARBECUE BEEF

BULGOGI

Bulgogi, literally 'fire meat' is a dish of thinly sliced grilled steak. The meat is marinated in a sweet soy, sesame and garlic sauce, which infuses it with a rich, savoury taste. While beef is the most common choice, bulgogi can also be made with chicken or pork. Dish pictured on page 95.

Serves 2-3   10 minutes plus marinating   6 minutes

INGREDIENTS
500g (1lb 2oz) rump (or sirloin) steak, thinly sliced
1 onion, sliced
Vegetable oil

For the marinade
80ml (2¾fl oz) soy sauce
40g (1½oz) brown sugar
30g (1oz) minced garlic
2 spring onions (scallion), finely chopped
1 tablespoon sesame oil
2 teaspoons ground black pepper
1 teaspoon toasted sesame seeds, plus extra to garnish

1. Mix the marinade ingredients together and use them to coat your sliced steak and sliced onion. Chill in the refrigerator for at least 1 hour (up to 24 hours).

2. Heat a little vegetable oil in a cast-iron pan over a medium-high heat and grill the slices of marinated beef and onion for 2–3 minutes on each side until the meat starts to turn brown or char.

3. To finish, plate it up and add a sprinkle of sesame seeds. To make a ssam, wrap the meat in leafy greens and dip in Ssamjang (see page 160).

KOREAN-STYLE BARBECUE BEEF, PAGE 93

SPICY STIR-FRIED PORK, PAGE 99

닭갈비

SPICY STIR-FRIED CHICKEN

DAK GALBI

Serves 2-3   10 minutes plus   15 minutes
               marinating

This is a flavour-packed dish, originating from Chuncheon in north-eastern South Korea, where boneless chicken thighs are marinated in a spicy sauce, along with sweet potatoes and other veggies. It is traditionally cooked over charcoal, giving it an amazing grilled flavour, but this stir-fried version is just as tasty!

INGREDIENTS

500g (1lb 2oz) skinless, boneless chicken thigh fillets, cut into bite-sized pieces
250g (9oz) sweet potato, sliced into rounds
1 tablespoon vegetable oil
1 onion, sliced
80g (2¾oz) white cabbage, cut into bite-sized pieces
200g (7oz) tteokbokki tteok (Korean rice cakes), optional
2 spring onions (scallions), chopped
2 red chilli peppers, sliced
1 tablespoon toasted sesame seeds
Pinch of ground black pepper

For the gochujang sauce

3 tablespoons gochujang
2 tablespoons coarse gochugaru
2 tablespoons soy sauce
1 tablespoon sugar
1 tablespoon honey
1 tablespoon minced garlic
1 tablespoon water
1 tablespoon sesame oil

1. Combine all the ingredients for the sauce in a large bowl. Add the chicken and sweet potato to the sauce then transfer to the refrigerator for at least 30 minutes to marinate.

2. Heat a large frying pan with the vegetable oil, then stir-fry the marinated chicken and sweet potatoes for around 5 minutes. Add the onion, cabbage and rice cakes (if using) once the sweet potatoes are about half-cooked. Stir-fry for about 5 minutes, adding a little water to the pan to help prevent burning.

3. Once the vegetables are cooked, add the spring onion (scallion), chilli peppers and sesame seeds and sprinkle with black pepper. Stir-fry for a further minute and then remove from the heat.

4. Serve hot from the pan. Wrap it in lettuce or perilla leaves.

☺ SEJI'S TIP

This is a versatile dish that can be enjoyed on its own or paired with a side of steamed rice. A popular tradition is to mix the leftovers and sauce with warm rice to create a delicious fried-rice dish.

등갈비강정

PORK RIBS WITH STICKY GOCHUJANG SAUCE

PORK GANGJEONG

I love pork ribs because of their juicy and tender meat. Typically enjoyed grilled or barbecued, another way to enjoy them is boiled, then baked in the oven and coated in sticky gochujang sauce. Perfect as a *banchan* (side dish) alongside a hearty meal or as a snack with beer.

Serves 2-3   5 minutes   40 minutes

INGREDIENTS
1.5kg (3lb 5oz) pork ribs
1.5 litres (3¼ pints) water
1 teaspoon black peppercorns
3 bay leaves
2 tablespoons doenjang

For the rub
½ teaspoon minced fresh root ginger
½ tablespoon minced garlic
½ teaspoon ground black pepper
1 tablespoon vegetable oil

For the sauce
2 tablespoons soy sauce
3 tablespoons water
½ tablespoon minced garlic
1 tablespoon sugar
1 tablespoon gochujang
1 tablespoon tomato ketchup
1 tablespoon honey
Pinch of ground black pepper
1 tablespoon coarse gochugaru

To garnish
Finely chopped chives
Peanuts, crushed

1. Put the ribs, measured water, peppercorns, bay leaves and doenjang in a large stockpot and boil for about 15 minutes. Remove the ribs from the pot and set aside to cool slightly.

2. Preheat the oven to 180°C fan/400°F/ gas mark 6. Line a baking tray with foil or baking paper.

3. Mix together the ingredients for the rub. Using your fingers, rub it over the ribs to cover all sides. Put the ribs on the lined tray and bake for 20 minutes until golden.

4. Meanwhile, put all the sauce ingredients into a pan over a medium heat. Once it boils, reduce the heat to medium-low, and add the baked pork ribs to the pan. Mix well until the sauce evenly coats the ribs.

5. Plate up and garnish with chopped chives and peanuts. Enjoy!

☺ SEJI'S TIP
It's important to boil the ribs first, as it really deepens the flavour.

제육 볶음

SPICY STIR-FRIED PORK

JEYUK BOKKEUM

You can find this dish in almost every Korean restaurant, and it's one that's truly loved by many: slices of tender pork belly or loin are marinated in a spicy, gochujang-based sauce. Serve with a bowl of The Perfect Steamed Rice (see page 48) and you have a full meal. Dish pictured on page 95.

Serves 2-3   10 minutes   15 minutes

INGREDIENTS

Vegetable oil, for stir-frying
500g (1lb 2oz) pork belly or loin, sliced
8 garlic cloves, sliced
2 spring onions (scallions), sliced into
 5cm (2in) lengths
1 onion, sliced
1 green chilli pepper, sliced
1 teaspoon salt
½ teaspoon ground black pepper
Toasted sesame seeds, ground, to
 garnish

For the sauce

3 tablespoons gochujang
2 tablespoons coarse gochugaru
2 tablespoons soy sauce
1 tablespoon sugar
1 tablespoon honey
1 tablespoon minced garlic
1 tablespoon sesame oil, plus extra to
 garnish
1 tablespoon water

1. Combine all the ingredients for the sauce in a bowl and set aside.

2. Heat some vegetable oil in a large frying pan, add the pork belly and fry over a medium heat for around 5–10 minutes, seasoning with salt and pepper to taste.

3. Once the juices start to run clear, add the garlic and fry until golden, about 1–2 minutes.

4. Add the spring onion (scallion), onion, chilli pepper and the sauce mixture and stir-fry until all the ingredients are sizzling and evenly coated in sauce. Add a little water to the pan if needed.

5. Once everything is cooked, drizzle over some sesame oil and mix again.

6. Plate up your jeyuk bokkeum, add a sprinkle of ground sesame seeds and tuck in!

엘에이 갈비

KOREAN-STYLE SHORT BEEF RIBS

LA GALBI

Serves 2-3   5 minutes plus   30 minutes
              marinating

INGREDIENTS
600g (1lb 5oz) beef short ribs, Korean
  cut

For the marinade
100ml (3½fl oz) soy sauce
250ml (9fl oz) water
40g (1½oz) sugar
1 tablespoon minced garlic
1 tablespoon minced fresh root ginger
2 spring onions (scallions), finely
  chopped
1 tablespoon sesame oil
1 teaspoon ground black pepper

Galbi, which means 'ribs' in Korean, originated in Los Angeles, California, as the name of this dish suggests. The uniqueness of LA galbi lies in the way the ribs are cut, about 1cm (½in) thick, across the rib bone from the chuck end of the rib. To achieve authentic LA galbi, ask your local butcher to cut the ribs for you.

This dish holds a special place in the hearts of those born and raised in Korea as it's often enjoyed when families gather for birthdays or holidays. While typically it's griddled in a pan, the below method uses the oven as a simple alternative.

1. First make the marinade by combining the soy sauce, water, sugar, garlic, ginger and spring onion (scallion) in a bowl. Mix well until the sugar is fully dissolved, then add the sesame oil and pepper.

2. Stack the ribs in layers in an airtight container then pour the marinade over them. Marinate the ribs in the sauce for at least 3–4 hours, or overnight in the refrigerator for best results.

3. Preheat the oven to 200°C fan/425°F/ gas mark 7. Place the ribs and the marinade on a baking tray lined with foil or baking paper. Cook for 25–30 minutes. Halfway through, flip the ribs for even cooking, and watch closely to avoid burning.

4. Place on a large dish. Serve with Coriander Kimchi Salad (see page 27) and a bowl of The Perfect Steamed Rice (see page 48).

서울

SEOUL FOOD & FUSION

With its never-ending energy, the vibrant city of Seoul is the perfect destination for late-night snacking on street food and *anju* or Korean tapas, best enjoyed alongside a cold glass of beer or, of course, soju: Korean's national drink.

My fusion recipes take the bold flavours of Korea's cuisine and twists them with Western favourites, such as gochujang spiked pasta (see pages 144–147); flavoursome, fermented aiolis (see pages 156 and 157); and even an umami-packed salted caramel cookie (see page 171).

STREET FOOD

간식

6

Korean street food injects a vibrant and exciting dimension into Korean cuisine. It's conveniently available at food stalls and vendors all over Seoul and South Korea, offering a diverse range of options.

If you're craving a savoury treat, you cannot miss the Korean Fried Chicken (see page 106), a true staple of the local food scene. Another popular choice among Seoul's street-food enthusiasts is the iconic Spicy Korean Rice Cakes, also known as tteokbokki (see page 113): a saucy dish that will warm your soul. You can find tteokbokki stalls all across the city, particularly in the bustling areas of Myeong-dong and Hongdae.

양념치킨

KOREAN FRIED CHICKEN 3 WAYS:
ORIGINAL, SPICY GOCHUJANG
& SWEET SOY

As you walk along the lively streets of Seoul, it's clear that chicken restaurants are everywhere. In fact, there are more chicken restaurants in South Korea alone than the number of McDonald's worldwide. Koreans have a serious love affair with chicken.

Now, here's a short backstory. The whole chicken craze in Korea can be traced back to the aftermath of the 1997 Asian financial crisis. Tons of people were left without jobs, and needed a way to make a living. They saw an opportunity in the fried chicken game because it didn't require a lot of money to get started. As you can imagine, this led to fierce competition, and every place wanted to stand out. That's why there's such a variety of chicken seasonings to choose from. Faced with all those tempting options, picking just one can be a real dilemma. But fear not! You can go for the half-and-half option – a popular choice in Korea for the best of both worlds.

Serves 2-3

10 minutes plus chilling

20 minutes

INGREDIENTS
1kg (2lb 4oz) chicken thigh fillets, skin on, cut into
 bite-sized pieces
Vegetable oil, for deep frying
Salt and ground black pepper

For the batter
500g (1lb 2oz) Korean fried chicken powder

OR make your own:
350g (12oz) plain (all-purpose) flour
30g (1oz) potato starch
2 tablespoons fine gochugaru (or ground paprika)
1 tablespoon ground black pepper
2 teaspoons salt
1½ teaspoons baking powder
1 teaspoon sugar

For Original Fried Chicken
Salt and ground black pepper

**For Spicy Gochujang Chicken,
 pictured on page 107**
50g (1¾oz) gochujang
180g (6oz) honey (or golden syrup)
80g (2¾oz) tomato ketchup
40g (1½oz) soy sauce
70g (2½oz) minced garlic
20g (¾oz) fine gochugaru
60g (2¼oz) sugar

For Sweet Soy Chicken
1 large spring onion (scallion), finely
 chopped
1 green chilli pepper, finely chopped
1 red chilli pepper, finely chopped
4 tablespoons soy sauce
½ tablespoon fish sauce
4 tablespoons sugar
1 tablespoon minced garlic
1 tablespoon rice wine vinegar
4 tablespoons plain (all-purpose)
 flour
1 tablespoon ground black pepper

To garnish
Crushed peanuts or toasted sesame
 seeds
Spring onion (scallion)
Red chilli pepper, sliced (optional)

1. Season the chicken thighs with salt and pepper, then leave to rest in the refrigerator for about 2 hours.

2. Combine your sauce ingredients in a bowl and mix thoroughly. Set aside.

3. Divide the Korean fried chicken powder into two separate bowls (if making your own: sift all the ingredients together then weigh off half into a separate bowl). Keep one half dry, and to the other, stir in 190ml (6¾fl oz) of water to make a wet batter.

4. Heat the oil in a deep-fat fryer or a large, heavy-based, deep-sided pan to 165–170°C (330–345°F) or until a cube of bread dropped into the hot oil browns in 30 seconds. Coat the chicken thigh pieces in wet batter then cover evenly in the dry mix. Carefully lower into the hot oil and fry for 7 minutes – do not overcrowd the pan, you may need to work in batches. After frying the chicken, lift out the pieces with a slotted spoon and allow to cool for a short period. Then fry again for 5 minutes. Repeat until all the chicken is cooked.

5. For the original version, Koreans love simply dipping fried chicken in a 1:1 ratio mixture of salt and pepper. To make the sauce for the other two types of chicken, add the ingredients for the version of your choice to a pan and mix. Heat over a medium heat until the sauce bubbles, then drizzle over the chicken to fully coat.

6. Transfer the chicken to a serving plate and garnish with peanuts or sesame seeds, spring onions (scallions) and chilli pepper, if using. Enjoy!

ADDITIONS TO KOREAN FRIED CHICKEN

In Korea, it is customary to accompany fried chicken with radish pickle, Korean-style salad, or a bowl of rice. While fried chicken is often savoured as a late-night snack, it can also make for a hearty meal with the following accompaniments.

GARLIC BUTTER RICE

Serves 2-3   10 minutes   30 minutes

INGREDIENTS
200g (7oz) The Perfect Steamed Rice
 (see page 48)
20 garlic cloves, peeled
2 tablespoons vegetable oil
30g (2 tablespoons) salted butter
½ teaspoon ground black pepper
Salt to taste

1. Prepare the rice according to the instructions on page 48. Tip into a bowl and keep warm.

2. Remove the ends of the garlic cloves and chop them to achieve a granular texture.

3. Heat the oil in a frying pan over a low heat. Add the garlic and a pinch of salt, then stir-fry the garlic, stirring constantly to prevent it from burning.

4. Once the garlic turns golden brown, remove it from the pan and drain any excess oil. Set the garlic aside.

5. Combine the warm rice, butter, pepper and garlic. Mix well until the butter melts and coats the rice. Taste and season with salt, if desired.

SHREDDED WHITE CABBAGE WITH SESAME MAYO DRESSING

Serves 2   5 minutes

INGREDIENTS
400g (14oz) white cabbage

For the dressing
8 tablespoons mayonnaise
4 tablespoons toasted sesame seeds
½ tablespoon soy sauce
1 tablespoon sugar
1 tablespoon honey
1 tablespoon lemon juice
1 spring onion (scallion)

1. Finely shred the white cabbage using a mandoline or the slicer attachment of a food processor.

2. Put all the dressing ingredients in a blender. Blend until smooth and well combined.

3. Trickle the sesame mayo dressing over the sliced cabbage.

쌈밥

CABBAGE LEAF WRAPS WITH TUNA SSAMJANG

SSAMBAP

Serves 2

5 minutes

20 minutes

Cabbage leaves are perfect for making healthy and delicious wrapped rice rolls. The leaves are blanched and wrapped around a savoury, salty mixture of rice and tuna ssamjang. This recipe is simple and nutritious, perfect for a healthy diet.

INGREDIENTS
8 savoy cabbage leaves
8 white cabbage leaves
400g (14oz) The Perfect Steamed Rice
  (see page 48), room temperature
Salt and sesame oil to taste

For the tuna ssamjang
2 tablespoons doenjang
1 tablespoon gochujang
1 tablespoon sesame oil
2 tablespoons Mayonnaise
½ tablespoon toasted sesame seeds
1 garlic clove, minced
145g (5oz) tinned tuna (I prefer tuna
  chunks in spring water)

1. Blanch the cabbage leaves in boiling water for 1 minute. Transfer them to a bowl of icy water to stop the cooking process, then drain and set aside.

2. Trim off the tough stems on the kale and cabbage leaves.

3. Mix the rice with salt and sesame oil in a large bowl.

4. To make the tuna ssamjang, whisk together the ingredients in a small bowl.

5. Take a spoonful of rice, make a small well in the middle, and spoon some tuna ssamjang dip into the rice ball. Place the rice ball in the centre of a leaf. Wrap tightly to form a roll. Repeat to make 16 wrapped rolls.

6. Wrap the finished rolls in clingfilm to help maintain their shape. Set aside for at least 30 minutes. Serve with extra dip on the side.

떡볶이

SPICY KOREAN RICE CAKES

TTEOKBOKKI

Serves 2-3   5 minutes   20 minutes

If you are looking for an authentic recipe to make with gochujang, spicy rice cakes or tteokbokki might be your best choice. This beloved street food is enjoyed by people of all ages: it's chewy, sweet, spicy and savoury. If you haven't had it before, think of it as a savoury mochi or maybe like gnocchi in a spicy sauce.

INGREDIENTS

800ml (1¾ pints) water
400g (14oz) tteokbokki tteok (Korean rice cakes)
100g (3½oz) white cabbage, sliced into bite-sized pieces
4 spring onions (scallions), sliced diagonally
100g (3½oz) Korean fish cake (or 6–8 fish balls), cut into bite-sized pieces
4 eggs, hard-boiled (optional)
Toasted sesame seeds

For the sauce

60g (2¼oz) gochujang
30g (1oz) coarse gochugaru
4 tablespoons sugar
3 tablespoons soy sauce
½ tablespoon fish sauce
1 tablespoon vegetable oil

1. Pour the measured water into a large pan, and stir in all the sauce ingredients. Add the rice cakes and boil over a medium-high heat, stirring occasionally, for about 8–10 minutes or until they become very soft and the sauce has thickened. Rice cakes vary, so you may need more time to reach a desired level of softness. Feel free to add more water as necessary.

2. Add the cabbage, spring onions (scallions) and fish cake, continue to boil, stirring constantly, for a further 4–6 minutes.

3. Finally, add the hard-boiled eggs, if using.

4. Transfer the tteokbokki to a serving dish and sprinkle sesame seeds on top.

GIMBAP – KOREAN SEAWEED RICE ROLLS

Gimbap, also known as kimbap, is a famous Korean dish where rice seasoned with sesame oil and salt, and an array of other ingredients, is rolled in a sheet of seaweed (gim).

While some may confuse gimbap with sushi rolls, it stands proudly as a traditional Korean food that has its own unique flavour profile and an interesting and long history. For Koreans, gimbap holds a special place in memories of school field-trip lunches. Also, it is a much-loved and convenient option for a simple meal.

Gimbap is a dish that welcomes creative substitutions and alternative choices, allowing you to curate a gimbap experience customized to your preferences. Traditional fillings offer a taste of familiarity, while simpler alternatives provide a quick and effortless dining experience.

Finding traditional fillings such as Korean pickled radish, lotus root, fish cake or gimbap ham may pose a challenge, but I have curated a collection of my favourite gimbap recipes that feature readily accessible ingredients, while still delivering the authentic Korean taste.

BEFORE YOU START TO MAKE GIMBAP

When it comes to the rice, opt for short-grain with slightly more water. This will result in rice that is slightly sticky, making it easier to roll into gimbap. For the perfect rice, follow the recipe on page 48.

As for the seaweed, choose larger Korean unseasoned gim, or seaweed sheets. If you can't find gim, you can substitute with sheets of nori.

Preparing fillings
The key here lies in slicing your ingredients into slender strips that span the length of the seaweed sheet. By doing so, you'll ensure a seamless roll. Don't forget to prepare all your fillings before you start to roll, as this will streamline the assembly process.

김밥

BASIC SEAWEED RICE ROLLS

GIMBAP

This very basic version is a great place to start making gimbap. Carrots, spinach and eggs take the spotlight as the main ingredients, but feel free to personalize your fillings based on your preferences. The possibilities are endless!

Serves 2-3   15 minutes   25 minutes

INGREDIENTS
3 unseasoned gim sheets
Vegetable oil
Sugar
Sesame oil
1 tablespoon toasted sesame seeds
Salt

For the rice
600g (1lb 5oz) The Perfect Steamed
 Rice (see page 48)
1 tablespoon salt
2 tablespoons sesame oil

For the filling
2 eggs
1 carrot, julienned
300g (10½oz) spinach
1 cucumber, seeds removed and cut
 lengthways
2 hot dogs, cut lengthways
4 seafood sticks, cut lengthways

Step 1: Season the rice

Put the cooked rice, salt and sesame oil in a large bowl and mix them evenly using a spatula. (If the rice is too hot, let it cool first slightly as hot rice can make the roll soggy.)

Step 2: Prepare the fillings

Eggs: Beat the eggs in a small bowl with a pinch of salt and sugar. Preheat a large nonstick frying pan with a little vegetable oil over a low heat. Pour the egg mixture into the pan and swirl it evenly to thinly cover the surface. Cook the egg into a very thin egg sheet, at a low heat, so there's no need to flip. Transfer to a board and let it cool. Cut lengthways into 2cm (¾in) wide strips. (Note: you can also scramble the eggs for an easy option.)

Carrot: Preheat a large nonstick frying pan with a little vegetable oil over a low heat. Add the julienned carrot and stir-fry with a pinch of salt for about 1 minute until slightly softened. Set aside to cool.

Spinach: Blanch the spinach in a pan of boiling water for about 10–15 seconds. Drain as soon as the leaves are wilted and plunge them into cold water. Squeeze out excess water and season with salt and sesame oil. Set aside.

Cucumber, hot dogs, seafood sticks: Preheat a large nonstick frying pan with a little vegetable oil over a low heat. Stir-fry the cucumbers, hot dogs and seafood sticks with a pinch of salt separately until just slightly softened – this takes about 1 minute. Set aside to cool.

Step 3: Assemble and roll

i. Place a seaweed sheet on a bamboo rolling mat. Spread the rice (about the size of a tennis ball) evenly and thinly to cover three-quarters of the sheet, leaving a gap of about 4cm (1½in) across the top of the sheet.

ii. Arrange the fillings in a line along the bottom edge of the rice-covered seaweed.

iii. Hold the ingredients together with your hands and tightly roll the seaweed. Seal the top end of the seaweed with a few drops of sesame oil.

iv. To finish, rub the surface of the rolled gimbap with a little more sesame oil, then sprinkle with sesame seeds for extra flavour. Cut it into bite-sized pieces using a sharp knife. Enjoy!

VARIATION: this type of gimbap features tuna mayonaise and it's no surprise that it's one of the most popular variations in Korea. Generally, tuna and fresh perilla leaves are used together for the filling, but I personally love rocket (arugula) leaves as an alternative to perilla.

200g (7oz) canned tuna, drained
2 tablespoons mayonnaise
Pinch of ground black pepper
Handful of rocket (arugula) leaves

1. Mix the tuna, mayonnaise and pepper in a bowl.

2. Assemble and roll following step iii above, sprinkling the rocket (arugula) leaves just before rolling the gimbap.

꼬마 김밥

MINI GIMBAP

KKOMA GIMBAP

This is a simpler version of gimbap, called kkoma gimbap or little gimbap. I enjoy it as it is, but in Korea I like to pair it with different street foods, such as tteokbokki. This cute little gimbap doesn't need to be cut into smaller sizes – pick it up whole with your hands and it will be gone in just one big bite!

Serves 2-3   5 minutes   5 minutes

INGREDIENTS
3 unseasoned gim sheets, cut into
 quarters (so 12 in total)
Vegetable oil
Sesame oil
1 tablespoon toasted sesame seeds
Salt

For the rice
600g (1lb 5oz) The Perfect Steamed
 Rice (see page 48)
1 teaspoon salt
2 tablespoons sesame oil

For the filling
300g (10½oz) spinach
1 carrot, julienned
2 yellow (bell) peppers, thinly sliced

Step 1: Season the rice
Follow Step 1 on page 118.

Step 2: Prepare the fillings
Spinach: Blanch the spinach in a pan of boiling water for about 10–15 seconds. Drain as soon as the leaves are wilted and plunge them into cold water. Squeeze out excess water and season with salt and sesame oil. Set aside.

Carrot and yellow pepper: Preheat a large nonstick frying pan with a little vegetable oil over medium heat. Stir-fry the carrot and pepper with a pinch of salt for about 1 minute until slightly softened. Set aside to cool.

Step 3: Assemble and roll
1. Place one of the quartered seaweed sheets on a bamboo rolling mat (or on a chopping board) with the shorter side toward you. Spread 50g (1¾oz) of the rice evenly and thinly to cover three-quarters of the sheet, leaving a gap of about 2cm (¾in) across the top of the sheet.

2. Continue assembling and rolling, using the instructions from step ii on page 118.

궁중떡볶이

'ROYAL COURT' KOREAN RICE CAKES

GUNGJUNG TTEOKBOKKI

Serves 2-3   5 minutes plus soaking   20 minutes

INGREDIENTS

250g (9oz) tteokbokki tteok (Korean rice cakes)
1 tablespoon vegetable oil
150g (5½oz) beef, any cut, sliced into strips
½ onion, sliced
½ carrot, julienned
½ green (bell) pepper, thinly sliced
½ red chilli pepper, thinly sliced
100g (3½oz) mushrooms (any variety of your choice)
Salt to taste

For the sauce

3 tablespoons soy sauce
1½ tablespoons sugar
½ teaspoon ground black pepper

To garnish

Sesame oil
Toasted sesame seeds
Ground black pepper

Originating from the illustrious Joseon dynasty, this dish was once part of the esteemed royal cuisine, renowned for its sophistication. This traditional version of tteokbokki – unlike its modern, fiery counterpart on page 113 – is delicately infused with soy sauce and has subtle sweetness and savoury notes. The preparation process and sauce are similar to that of japchae (see page 62).

1. If your rice cakes are not soft, soak them in warm water for 10 minutes, then drain.

2. Combine the sauce ingredients in a bowl. Set aside.

3. Heat the oil in a large frying pan over a medium-high heat and add the beef. Stir-fry while lightly sprinkling with salt, for around 3 minutes.

4. When the meat is half-cooked, add the sauce and tteokbokki tteok (Korean rice cakes). Continue to stir-fry for a further 2–3 minutes. If desired, add a little water to adjust the consistency.

5. Add all the vegetables and mushrooms to the pan and stir-fry for a final 2–3 minutes.

6. Serve with a drizzle of sesame oil and sprinkled with sesame seeds. Add some ground black pepper for extra flavour.

핫도그

KOREAN CORN DOGS

GAMJA HOTDOG

 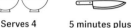

Serves 4 | 5 minutes plus proving | 10 minutes

INGREDIENTS
4 jumbo hot dog sausages
120g (4½oz) panko breadcrumbs
Vegetable oil
White granulated sugar
Gochujang Ketchup (see page 155), to
  serve

For the dough
250g (9oz) plain (all-purpose) flour
100ml (3½fl oz) milk
1 egg
2 tablespoons sugar
1 teaspoon salt
1 teaspoon baking powder

A much-loved street food that has become a worldwide sensation, Korean corn dogs are a savoury and slightly sweet treat featuring a hot dog sausage in a crisp panko breadcrumb coating.

1. Spear each sausage lengthways with a wooden skewer, so there is around 10cm (4in) of the skewer sticking out.

2. Combine the dough ingredients in a large bowl. Thoroughly mix together, then leave at room temperature for 1 hour to allow the dough to rise. The consistency of the mixture should be somewhere between that of a batter and a dough, leaning closer to the dough's texture – thick and sticky.

3. Once the dough has risen, evenly coat your skewered sausages with dough. For ease, place the dough in a long glass for easy coating and dunk the sausage in the glass. The batter should adhere to the skewers without dripping off easily.

4. Spread the panko breadcrumbs on a tray lined with baking paper and gently roll the dough-coated skewers, shaping them around the sausage as you go.

5. Heat the vegetable oil in a deep pan (allow enough to cover the corn dogs) to 175°C (340°F) or until a cube of bread dropped into the hot oil browns in 30 seconds. Carefully lower the corn dogs into the hot oil and fry for about 5–6 minutes until golden and crispy.

6. Using tongs, remove the corn dogs from the pan and let them drain on a wire rack.

7. Sprinkle white sugar over the corn dogs and drizzle with Gochujang Ketchup.

☺ **SEJI'S TIP**
These also go well with Kimchi Aioli (see page 157).

닭꼬치

GOCHUJANG CHICKEN SKEWERS

DAK KKOCHI

8
Makes 8
skewers

5 minutes
plus resting

20 minutes

INGREDIENTS
500g (1lb 2oz) chicken thigh fillets,
 skin on, cut into bite-sized pieces
Vegetable oil
6 spring onions (scallions), cut into
 4cm (1½in) lengths
10g (¼oz) finely chopped chives
Salt and ground black pepper

For the gochujang sauce
1 tablespoon gochujang
1½ tablespoons tomato ketchup
1 tablespoon coarse gochugaru
2 tablespoons honey
1 tablespoon soy sauce
½ tablespoon minced garlic
½ teaspoon ground black pepper

Everything tastes better on skewers, right? When it comes to street food in Korea, chicken skewers are a go-to choice. These skewers, coated in a sweet and spicy gochujang sauce, are great for any party menu and incredibly quick and easy to prepare.

1. Begin by seasoning the chicken pieces with salt and pepper, then leave to rest for about 10 minutes. Meanwhile, make the sauce by mixing all the ingredients in a bowl. Set aside.

2. Preheat a large frying pan then grease with a little oil. Add the chicken pieces (in batches if need be) to the pan and cook until golden brown on all sides. Once cooked, transfer the pieces to a separate plate while you cook the rest.

3. Thread the chicken and spring onion alternately onto 8 metal skewers. Repeat until you've used up all your chicken and spring onion. Brush the gochujang sauce on the chicken skewers.

4. Place the chicken skewers on a heated flat griddle pan with little vegetable oil and cook over a medium-low heat for about 3–5 minutes. Turn and cook for a further 3–5 minutes. Brush the remaining sauce onto the chicken skewers, transfer to a baking tray and grill under a medium-high heat until cooked thoroughly.

5. Sprinkle with chopped chives to add a finishing touch. Enjoy!

☺ **SEJI'S TIP**
While the classic version uses chicken and spring onion (scallion), you can swap the spring onions for rice cakes for an even more satisfying bite.

라면

RAMYEON – IT'S NOT RAMEN!
CHILLED RAMYEON WITH CUCUMBER

Serves 1   5 minutes   5 minutes

INGREDIENTS
550ml (1¼ pints) water
1 packet ramyeon with flavour packet
 (without using the vegetable packet)
150g (5½oz) bean sprouts
20g (¾oz) cucumber, thinly sliced
1 fried egg (optional)
½ tablespoon white wine vinegar
Toasted sesame seeds

For the sauce
The flavour packet from the ramyeon
 packet
½ tablespoon coarse gochugaru
½ tablespoon gochujang
1 tablespoon sugar
1 tablespoon sesame oil
2 tablespoons vegetable oil

Do you have instant Korean noodles in your cupboard? They're convenient to have, but why settle for a basic bowl when you can jazz it up in under 10 minutes? Get ready for three super-easy ramyeon hacks that will transform your noodles into something extraordinary.

Prepare to be captivated by this addictive spicy bowl of chilled ramyeon!

1. Start by preparing the sauce. Combine all the ingredients except the vegetable oil in a heatproof bowl and mix thoroughly. Heat the oil in a small pan over a medium heat, ensuring it doesn't reach smoking point. Carefully pour the hot oil into the sauce bowl, allowing it to sizzle and infuse the mixture with aromas. Stir well then set aside to cool.

2. Bring the measured water to the boil in a pan. Add the ramen noodles and cook for 3 minutes over a high heat. Then add the bean sprouts to the pot and continue boiling for a further 1 minute.

3. Tip into a colander (strainer) and rinse the cooked ramyeon and bean sprouts with cold water to cool them down. Allow them to drain thoroughly.

4. Transfer the cooked ramyeon and bean sprouts to a serving bowl. Pour the prepared sauce over the noodles, and top with cucumber slices and a fried egg, if using. Sprinkle with the white vinegar and sesame seeds for an extra burst of flavour.

5. It's time to bibim (mix) it! Toss all the ingredients together until well combined. Enjoy!

SESAME EGG RAMYEON

 Serves 1 5 minutes 5 minutes

Koreans are fond of the classic combination of instant ramyeon and egg and here I've added a drizzle of sesame oil for a savoury twist.

INGREDIENTS
550ml (1¼ pints) water
1 packet ramyeon with flavour packet
 (without using the vegetable packet)
2 eggs, well beaten
1 tablespoon sesame oil

To garnish
Finely chopped chives
Toasted sesame seeds

1. Bring the measured water to the boil in a pan. Add the noodles and the flavour packet, and cook for 4 minutes over medium-high heat.

2. Add the beaten eggs to the pan and continue stirring for 20 seconds. The eggs will create a creamy texture in the ramyeon.

3. Transfer the ramyeon to a serving bowl and drizzle with sesame oil, garnish with chives and sesame seeds.

CREAMY RAMYEON

 Serves 1 5 minutes 5 minutes

If you're a fan of creamy sauces, this ramyeon is perfect for you.

INGREDIENTS
1 packet ramyeon with flavour packet
 (without using the vegetable packet)
350ml (12fl oz) milk
2–4 prawns (shrimp), peeled
2–4 mushrooms, sliced
½ tablespoon coarse gochugaru
½ spring onion (scallion), finely chopped

To garnish
Ground black pepper
Crushed chilli flakes
Grated (shredded) Parmesan cheese
 (optional)

1. Bring a pan of water to the boil. Add the noodles and cook for 1–2 minutes then turn off the heat and quickly drain them.

2. Pour the milk into the empty pan, add the drained noodles along with the flavour packet. Stir well and continue cooking over a medium heat for a further minute.

3. As the mixture begins to form a creamy soup, add the prawns (shrimp), mushrooms, gochugaru, and spring onion (scallion). Cook for 5–7 minutes.

4. Transfer the ramyeon in a bowl, garnish with pepper, chilli and Parmesan, if using.

FAR RIGHT, SESAME EGG RAMYEON, PAGE 127

RIGHT, CREAMY RAMYEON, PAGE 127

BELOW, CHILLED RAMYEON WITH CUCUMBER, PAGE 126

통닭

CHICKEN STUFFED WITH STICKY RICE & GARLIC

TONGDAK

Serves 1–2   15 minutes plus resting   1 hour 45 minutes

S
T
R
E
E
T

F
O
O
D

INGREDIENTS

1 extra-small whole chicken (about 1kg/2lb 4oz)
200g (7oz) short-grain rice (or pudding rice)
5–6 garlic cloves, peeled
Olive oil
Salt and ground black pepper to taste

For the honey gochujang dip

2–3 garlic cloves, minced
2 tablespoons gochujang
2 tablespoons tomato ketchup
2 tablespoons honey

This whole chicken dish is prepared using traditional Korean roasting techniques. Succulent chicken is stuffed with sticky rice and garlic, infusing every bite with an explosion of Korean flavours.

1. Trim any excess fat from the inside of the chicken, ensuring it is clean and dry. Season with salt and pepper, then place the bird in the refrigerator for a few hours.

2. Preheat the oven to 200°C fan/425°F/ gas mark 7, then rinse the rice and soak it in cold water for about 10 minutes.

3. Stuff the chicken with the soaked rice and garlic, then tie the chicken legs with kitchen string or close the opening with skewers.

4. Coat the chicken with olive oil and place it breast-side up on a rack in a roasting tin in the oven.

5. Roast the chicken for about 1 hour or until it is fully cooked and the stuffing is heated through. Then turn the heat down to 175°C fan/380°F/gas mark 5 and cook for a further 45 minutes.

6. Meanwhile, mix the ingredients for the honey gochujang dip in a small bowl and set aside.

7. Serve the chicken with the gochujang dip, alongside Cubed Pickled Radish (see page 22) or a refreshing Shredded White Cabbage with Sesame Mayo Dressing (see page 109).

TAPAS & TWISTS

7

In Korea, the concept of *anju* or tapas is more than just a few small side dishes – it's any type of food that is consumed alongside alcoholic drinks, and refers to a variety of dishes, including both mains and sides.

This chapter contains modern dishes inspired by present-day Seoul, which combine elements of fusion cuisine, such as my Oven-baked Kimchi Pancakes (see page 142) and Gochujang Butter Bucatini (see page 149). All the dishes in this chapter perfectly complement alcoholic drinks such as *makgeolli* (rice wines), soju, beer, and other Korean liquors.

배추구이

ROAST CABBAGE WITH SSAMJANG AIOLI

BAECHUGU-I

Serves 3–4   5 minutes   40 minutes

INGREDIENTS

1 Chinese cabbage, cut into wedges
1 tablespoon crushed chilli flakes
100g (3½oz) salted butter, at room
  temperature
2 tablespoons extra virgin olive oil
¼ tablespoon sea salt (if using
  unsalted butter)

To serve

Chives, finally chopped
Crushed chilli flakes
Ssamjang Aioli (see page 156)

This is a great dish for any dinner party or special occasion: tender, tasty cabbage roasted to perfection and served with my bold and nutty Ssamjang Aioli.

1. Preheat the oven to 180°C fan/400°F/ gas mark 6.

2. Mix together the butter, oil and salt (if using) until smooth and creamy. Brush the spread evenly over the cabbage wedges.

3. Put the cabbage wedges on a baking tray and roast for about 30–35 minutes until golden brown and tender.

4. When the cabbage is roasted, remove the tray from the oven and set aside for 5 minutes.

5. Plate the cabbage wedges, and sprinkle the chives and chilli flakes on top. Serve with Ssamjang Aioli.

초계무침

SESAME-DRESSED CHICKEN & CUCUMBER SALAD

CHOGYE MUCHIM

Serves 2 | 5 minutes plus salting | 15 minutes

INGREDIENTS
1 cucumber, sliced
360ml (12½fl oz) water
300g (10½oz) skinless chicken breast fillet
1 spring onion (scallion), roughly chopped
2 garlic cloves, peeled
Salt and ground black pepper

For the sesame dressing
1 tablespoon soy sauce
2 tablespoons white wine vinegar
2 tablespoons sugar
½ tablespoon toasted sesame seeds
1 tablespoon Dijon mustard
1 teaspoon minced garlic
1 teaspoon sesame oil

Tender chicken, crisp cucumber and an aromatic sesame dressing come together perfectly for a quick, light lunch.

1. Begin by sprinkling a dash of salt over the cucumber slices, then place in a colander (strainer). Allow to drain for about 20 minutes, then gently squeeze out any remaining water.

2. Pour the measured water into a pan and bring to the boil. Add the chicken breast, spring onion (scallion), garlic, and a pinch each of salt and black pepper. Simmer over a medium-high heat for about 15 minutes. Meanwhile, whisk together the ingredients for the sesame dressing.

3. Once the chicken is cooked, remove it from the pan, leave to cool then shred it into bite-sized pieces using your hands.

4. Place the shredded chicken and cucumber slices in a mixing bowl, gently tossing them in the sesame dressing. Transfer to the refrigerator to chill, allowing the flavours to develop. Serve chilled.

해물파전

RAINY-DAY SEAFOOD PANCAKE

HAEMUL PAJEON

In South Korea, we love to eat this savoury pancake when it rains. There are a few theories as to why this dish is so popular during downpours, but my favourite is that the sizzling of the pancakes in the pan sounds just like heavy raindrops.

Serves 2   5 minutes   7 minutes

INGREDIENTS

6 spring onions (scallions), cut into 10cm (4in) lengths
200g (7oz) mixed seafood (squid and prawn/shrimp)
2 green chilli peppers, sliced
3 tablespoons vegetable oil, plus extra as needed
2 eggs, beaten
1 red chilli pepper, sliced

For the dipping sauce
2 tablespoons soy sauce
1 tablespoon rice wine vinegar
1 tablespoon finely chopped onion

For the batter
100g (3½oz) plain (all-purpose) flour
½ tablespoon baking powder
½ tablespoon salt
Ground black pepper
160ml (scant 6fl oz) water

☺ SEJI'S TIP

For an even easier batter, you can also substitute the dry ingredients for 100g (3½oz) Korean pancake powder.

1. First mix the ingredients for the dipping sauce in a small bowl and set aside.

2. Next, make the pancake batter. Sift the flour, baking powder, salt and pepper into a large bowl and whisk in the water to form a smooth batter.

3. Gently stir through the spring onions (scallions), seafood and green pepper, making sure everything is coated.

4. Heat the oil in a large nonstick frying pan over a medium-high heat and swirl the pan until the base is fully covered and the oil is sizzling. Pour the batter evenly into the pan.

5. When the base is cooked (after about 2–3 minutes) pour the beaten eggs evenly over the top of the pancake, and garnish with the red chilli pepper.

6. Flip the pancake and continue to do so, adding more oil as needed, until the pancake is browned and crisp on both sides and the seafood is thoroughly cooked.

7. Transfer to a large plate and serve with the dipping sauce.

호박전

KOREAN-STYLE FRITTERS

HOBAK JEON

Serves 2

10 minutes
plus resting

20 minutes

INGREDIENTS

250g (9oz) potatoes, finely grated
  (shredded)
100g (3½oz) courgette (zucchini),
  julienned
1 red chilli pepper, finely chopped
2 tablespoons plain (all-purpose)
  flour
1 teaspoon fine salt
20g (¾oz) bacon crumble (optional)
Ground black pepper
Vegetable oil
Korean Soy Sauce Vinegar Dip, to
  serve (see page 160)

These potato and courgette (zucchini) fritters are crisp on the outside, soft and warm on the inside. They make the perfect comfort snack or can be paired with some fizz as a great addition to a Korean tapas menu.

1. Put all the ingredients (except the oil and dip) in a large bowl and stir to thoroughly combine. Leave for 10 minutes to allow the vegetables to release their water – this will help with cohesion of the mixture.

2. Place a large nonstick frying pan over a medium heat and add enough vegetable oil to coat the base of the pan.

3. Working in batches to avoid overcrowding the pan, place spoonfuls of the mixture in the pan, spreading it evenly to form fritter shapes. You should have enough batter for 4–5 fritters.

4. Cook the fritters for 3–4 minutes on each side, or until golden brown and crispy.

5. Transfer the cooked fritters to a serving plate and repeat the process with the remaining mixture.

6. Serve hot with the dipping sauce.

☺ SEJI'S TIP

For a twist on the traditional soy dipping sauce, you can also serve these fritters with a dollop of Greek yogurt or soured cream and a sprinkling of chives, as shown opposite. This combination adds a touch of sweetness and acidity that complements the fritters.

김치전

OVEN-BAKED KIMCHI PANCAKES

KIMCHI JEON

Serves 4   5 minutes   25 minutes

These bite-sized kimchi pancakes are sure to be a hit at your next party or gathering, plus they're simple to make and bake in a cupcake tray, leaving you with more time to enjoy the company of your guests. Alternatively, you can cook in batches in a nonstick frying pan, as with the other *jeons* (see pages 138 and 141). It's a good recipe for repurposing a batch of aged kimchi which is starting to go soft.

INGREDIENTS
500g (1lb 2oz) aged kimchi
3 tablespoons kimchi juice
1 tablespoon fine gochugaru
80g (2¾oz) spring onions (scallions), finely sliced, plus extra to garnish
Vegetable oil
2 red chilli peppers, thinly sliced

For the batter
450g (1lb) plain (all-purpose) flour
4 teaspoons baking powder
2 tablespoon salt
1 tablespoon sugar
600ml (1¼ pints) water

☺ SEJI'S TIP
For an even easier batter, you can also substitute the dry ingredients for 450g (1lb) Korean pancake powder.

1. Preheat the oven to 170°C fan/375°F/gas mark 5.

2. To make the pancake batter, sift the flour, baking powder, salt and sugar into a large bowl and whisk in the water to form a smooth batter.

3. Next, add the chopped kimchi, kimchi juice, gochugaru and spring onions (scallions) to the batter, and mix well to combine.

4. To ensure crispy edges, pour 1 tablespoon of vegetable oil into each hole of a 12-hole cupcake tray, then spoon the batter into the tray, filling each hole about three-quarters full. Add a slice of red chilli on top of each for a pop of colour.

5. Bake for 20–25 minutes or until the pancakes are golden brown and crispy on the outside. Remove from the oven and leave to cool for a few minutes. Use a fork or a knife to gently loosen the kimchi pancakes from the tray.

6. To serve, garnish the pancakes with extra chopped spring onions (scallions) and serve with a side of soy sauce or your favourite dipping sauce.

고추장참치라구

GOCHUJANG TUNA RAGÙ WITH RIGATONI

Tuna spiked with smoky gochujang creates a superb sauce that complements chunky rigatoni. A perfect meal for a busy weeknights that you can put on the table in less than half an hour.

Serves 2

5 minutes

20 minutes

INGREDIENTS
½ tablespoon olive oil
½ small onion, finely chopped
1 celery stick, finely chopped
150g (5½oz) canned tuna, drained
1 tablespoon coarse gochugaru
2 teaspoons minced garlic
1 teaspoon ground black pepper
200ml (7fl oz) water
1 tablespoon gochujang
150g (5½oz) rigatoni

To garnish
Finely chopped parsley
Crushed chilli flakes

1. Set a large frying pan over a medium heat and add the olive oil, onion and celery. Stir-fry lightly for 5 minutes.

2. Lower the heat and add the tuna, gochugaru, garlic and black pepper, and quickly stir-fry for a further 1–2 minutes.

3. Pour the measured water into the pan, add the gochujang and simmer over a low heat for 10 minutes.

4. Meanwhile, cook the rigatoni until al dente in a large pan of boiling water following the packet instructions. Drain the pasta, reserving 100ml (3½fl oz) of the pasta water.

5. Add the cooked rigatoni and reserved pasta water to the tuna ragù and stir for a final 2 minutes.

6. Plate up your pasta and sprinkle with chopped parsley and crushed chilli flakes.

☺ **SEJI'S TIP**
This tuna ragù sauce can also be paired with steamed rice to make a simple tuna bibimbap. Just remember to mix it all well together.

로제파스타

SPICY ROSÉ PASTA WITH PRAWNS

Rosé sauce is a new Korean favourite, known for its gentle spiciness and velvety creaminess. This pink pasta gets its colour from gochujang and gochugaru.

Serves 2   5 minutes   25 minutes

INGREDIENTS

150g (5½oz) rigatoni (or your choice of pasta or potato gnocchi)
1 tablespoon olive oil
½ onion, finely chopped
2 garlic cloves, minced
200ml (7fl oz) double (heavy) cream
200ml (7fl oz) milk
1 chicken stock (bouillon) cube, crumbled
½ tablespoon sugar
150g (5½oz) prawns (shrimp), peeled
1 tablespoon gochujang
2 tablespoons coarse gochugaru
Salt and ground black pepper

To garnish

Grated (shredded) Parmesan cheese
Finely chopped parsley
Crushed chilli flakes (optional)

1. First cook the rigatoni in a large pan of boiling water following the packet instructions until al dente. Once cooked, drain the pasta, reserving some of the pasta water.

2. Heat the oil in a pan over a medium heat, add the onion and sauté for 4–5 minutes until softened. Add the garlic and continue to cook for a further 1 minute.

3. Pour the cream and milk into the pan. Add the stock (bouillon) cube and sugar, and season with salt and pepper to taste. Allow the mixture to simmer for a few minutes.

4. Add the prawns (shrimp), gochujang and gochugaru to the pan. Stir well to combine all the ingredients. Let the sauce simmer, uncovered, over a low-medium heat until it becomes thick and creamy, stirring every now and then.

5. Add the cooked pasta and stir through the sauce to coat evenly. If the sauce appears too thick, add a splash of the reserved pasta water.

6. Transfer the pasta to 2 aserving dishes and garnish with some Parmesan, parsley and chilli flakes, if using. Enjoy immediately.

고추장버터 부가티니

GOCHUJANG BUTTER BUCATINI

This spicy sausage spaghetti dish takes you on a culinary journey from Italy to Korea via Japan. Inspired by the beloved Japanese Napolitan pasta, this recipe features sausages, ketchup and onion. But what sets it apart is the fiery kick of gochujang, adding a burst of incredible flavour to this simple dish.

 Serves 2    5 minutes   15 minutes

INGREDIENTS
150g (5½oz) bucatini
30g (2 tablespoons) butter
100g (3½oz) your favourite sausage,
 sliced
½ onion, sliced
4 garlic cloves, minced
Salt and ground black pepper

For the sauce
2 tablespoons gochujang
2 tablespoons tomato ketchup
1 teaspoon sugar (optional)
2 teaspoons Worcestershire sauce (or
 soy sauce)
1 tablespoon milk

1. First cook the bucatini in a large pan of boiling water following the packet instructions until al dente. Once cooked, drain the pasta, reserving some of the pasta water.

2. Meanwhile, make the sauce by stirring all the ingredients together in a small bowl. Set aside.

3. Heat a large frying pan over a medium heat, add the butter and stir-fry the sausage, onion and garlic. Season with salt and pepper.

4. Once the onion starts to caramelize, add the gochujang sauce mixture and stir together. Continue to cook until the sauce boils.

5. Add the bucatini and stir-fry for about 1–2 minutes. Check the seasoning and then add a little of the reserved pasta water.

6. Transfer the gochujang bucatini to plates and serve.

샐러드

KOREAN-STYLE POTATO SALAD

SALADA

Serves 4   20 minutes plus pickling   10 minutes

T
A
P
A
S

&

T
W
I
S
T
S

INGREDIENTS

⅓ cucumber, thinly sliced
½ small onion, finely chopped
½ small carrot, finely chopped
700g (1lb 9oz) potatoes, peeled and
  cut into 1cm (½in) cubes
1 apple, cored and finely sliced
20g (¾oz) dried cranberries
2 hard-boiled eggs, yolks and whites
  separated, whites roughly chopped
4 seafood sticks, sliced into small
  pieces
Salt

For the sauce

150g (5½oz) mayonnaise
½ tablespoon Dijon mustard
1 tablespoon white wine vinegar
2 tablespoons sugar
1 tablespoon soured cream (optional)
Salt and ground black pepper, to
  taste

This potato salad is similar to the classic version but with an extra crunch and freshness from apples and salted cucumbers. Salada is something Koreans love to have – as a *banchan* (side dish) or as a sandwich filling. It's the perfect accompaniment to Korean tapas, especially when paired with a glass of fizz and served alongside crackers – absolutely delicious!

1. Put the chopped cucumber, onion and carrot in a bowl and coat them evenly with salt. Leave to pickle for 20–25 minutes then tightly squeeze the water out of the vegetables.

2. Bring a pan of salted water to the boil and add the potatoes. Cook until tender then drain in a colander (strainer). Set aside until cool.

3. Meanwhile, make the sauce by stirring all the ingredients together in a jug or bowl.

4. Once cool, combine the cooked potatoes with the sliced apple, cranberries and chopped egg whites and pickled vegetables. Add the mayo sauce and gently mix everything together.

5. Grate the egg yolks over the salad to garnish, then serve.

☺ SEJI'S TIP

Add cooked macaroni to turn this into a pasta salad. Or, if you prefer a slightly sweeter taste, you can add some sweetcorn kernels.

케일 샐러드

KALE SALAD

Serves 2   10 minutes

Fresh, nutty and totally tasty, this simple salad is a breeze to put together and ready in under 10 minutes!

INGREDIENTS
120g (4½oz) curly or lacinato kale, leaves stripped from the thick stems and cut into small pieces
4 tablespoons Ssamjang Aioli (see page 156)
20g (¾oz) toasted walnuts (or pine nuts)
1 tablespoon toasted sesame seeds

1. Wash then dry the kale on paper towels. Put into a medium-large bowl and, using your hands, massage the kale until the leaves darken in colour and become tender.

2. Drizzle the Ssamjang over the kale, add most of the walnuts and toss to coat evenly.

3. Transfer the salad to a serving plate and top with remaining toasted walnuts and the sesame seeds, for texture and extra nuttiness. Enjoy right away while the topping is still perfectly crispy.

☺ SEJI'S TIP
To toast walnuts, heat in a dry frying pan over a medium-high heat, stirring frequently, until lightly toasted.

그린빈 샐러드

GREEN BEAN SALAD

Serves 4   5 minutes   5 minutes

This dish can be prepared ahead and served cold, making it a great choice for dinner parties as a side dish.

INGREDIENTS
200g (7oz) green beans, trimmed
4 tablespoons Ssamjang Aioli (see page 156)
10g (⅓oz) dill, finely chopped
10g (⅓oz) mint, finely chopped
10g (⅓oz) coriander (cilantro), finely chopped
Lemon zest, to garnish

1. Bring a pan of lightly salted water to the boil. Add the beans and boil for about 3–5 minutes until they are tender-crisp and still bright green.

2. Drain the beans well and immediately transfer them to a bowl of iced water to stop the cooking process. Drain again.

3. In a separate bowl, combine the blanched beans with the sauce. Add the herbs and toss well, garnish with some lemon zest before serving.

☺ SEJI'S TIP
Instead of beans, you can also use blanched asparagus or sautéed onions. Serve on toasted sourdough bread for a delicious breakfast.

SEJI'S SAUCES

세지네 소스비법

8

Korean sauces are rooted in *jang* – fermented pastes that all boast an irresistible flavour profile. The three *jangs* in Korean cuisine are gochujang, doenjang (soybean paste) and gangjang (soy sauce).

In this chapter, there are ideas and inspiration for you to easily incorporate the flavour of these *jangs* into your everyday meals, for instance by dressing a salad with Gochujang Vinaigrette (see page 160), dipping your chips (fries) into Ssamjang Aioli (see page 156) or spreading Gochujang Cream Cheese (see page 155) on your morning bagel.

쌈장

SOYBEAN SAUCE

SSAMJANG

The secret to this sauce's popularity is that it goes well with everything. It's sweet, creamy and savoury all at once. Typically eaten alongside Korean barbecue dishes, I also love to use it as a dip or to marinate meat and veggies, and dress salads. How you use it is up to you!

Serves 3-4   3 minutes

1. Whisk everything together until combined.

2. Put the sauce in an airtight container, store it in the refrigerator and use within a month.

INGREDIENTS
2 tablespoons doenjang
1 tablespoon gochujang
1 tablespoon sesame oil
2 tablespoons honey
½ tablespoon toasted sesame seeds
1 garlic clove, minced

고추장 케

GOCHUJANG KETCHUP

Serves 3-4   5 minutes

This is the ultimate mash up, the OG ketchup you love blended with gochujang for an extra kick! Use to accompany chips (fries) or burgers to elevates the ordinary to the extraordinary.

INGREDIENTS
300g (10½oz) tomato ketchup
100g (3½oz) gochujang
1 tablespoon golden syrup (or dark
 corn syrup)
1 teaspoon finely minced garlic
½ tablespoon soy sauce

1. Mix the ketchup, gochujang and golden syrup (corn syrup) in a bowl until they are well combined.

2. Add the garlic and soy sauce and mix to incorporate. Taste and adjust the seasoning as needed.

3. Put the sauce in an airtight container, store it in the refrigerator and use within a month.

☺ SEJI'S TIP
This sweet spicy dip is the perfect companion for roast or fried chicken.

고추장 크림 치즈

GOCHUJANG CREAM CHEESE WITH SUN-DRIED TOMATOES

Serves 3-4   3 minutes

Cream cheese and sun-dried tomatoes are transformed by sweet and spicy gochujang. This spread works well on bagels for brunch – or try it on toast, as a sandwich filling, or as a dip for chips (fries) or veggies.

INGREDIENTS
150g (5½oz) cream cheese
100g (3½oz) sun-dried tomatoes,
 finely chopped
1 tablespoon gochujang
2 tablespoons honey

1. Combine the ingredients in a bowl, mixing with a spatula until everything is well combined.

2. You can use immediately or store the dip in the refrigerator for 2–3 days.

약고추장

GOCHUJANG SAUCE

YAK-GOCHUJANG

Serves 3-4   5 minutes   15 minutes

S
E
J
I
S

S
A
U
C
E
S

This sauce is perfect for dipping crisp vegetables into, or alongside rice, noodles, or even bibimbap.

INGREDIENTS
1 tablespoon sesame oil
4 tablespoons vegetable oil
160g (5¾oz) onions, finely chopped
1 spring onion (scallion), finely chopped
30g (1oz) minced garlic
60g (2¼oz) minced (ground) beef
1 tablespoon soy sauce
1 tablespoon sugar
1 tablespoon honey
220g (7½oz) gochujang

1. Heat the oils in a frying pan over a medium heat. Add the onion, spring onion (scallion), garlic and beef and stir-fry for 7–8 minutes until the beef turns brown.

2. Once the beef is cooked, add the soy sauce and sugar. Stir-fry for 2–3 minutes.

3. Reduce the heat to low, add the honey and gochujang and gently stir-fry for 5 minutes, ensuring everything is mixed.

4. Allow to cool then put in an airtight container. Store in the refrigerator for 3–4 weeks (the fermented gochujang increases the shelf life of the beef).

쌈장 아욜리

SSAMJANG AIOLI

Serves 3-4   3 minutes

With a creamy texture and umami flavour, this aioli is an easy way to elevate salads, and also makes a fantastic dip for fresh or grilled vegetables

INGREDIENTS
4 tablespoons Ssamjang (Soybean Sauce, see page 154) or 3 tablespoons doenjang and 1 tablespoon gochujang
8 tablespoons mayonnaise
2 tablespoons rice vinegar
2 tablespoons lemon juice
2 tablespoons honey
1 tablespoon sesame oil
2 garlic cloves, minced

1. Whisk together the Ssamjang (or doenjang and gochujang) and mayonnaise in a small bowl to create a luscious and smooth creamy base.

2. Add the rest of the ingredients, whisking until everything is well combined. If it is too thick, add a little bit of water to thin the dressing to your desired consistency.

3. Put the sauce in an airtight container, store it in the refrigerator and use within a month.

김치 아욜리

KIMCHI AIOLI

Serves 3-4   5 minutes

Creamy, tangy and packed with umami – this condiment works well as a dip for fresh vegetables, crackers, tacos or chips (fries), or simply spread it on sandwiches, burgers or wraps.

INGREDIENTS
230g (8oz) mayonnaise
2 garlic cloves, minced
100g (3½oz) kimchi, chopped
1 tablespoon kimchi juice
1 tablespoon lemon juice
½ tablespoon sugar
½ tablespoon honey
¼ teaspoon salt
½ tablespoon sesame oil

1. Whisk together all the ingredients except the sesame oil in a bowl until well combined.

2. Add the oil to the bowl and whisk again until well combined.

3. Cover the bowl and refrigerate for at least 30 minutes before serving. This allows the flavours to meld and intensify.

4. Put the sauce in an airtight container, store it in the refrigerator and use within a month.

두부된장

TOFU DOENJANG DIP

Serves 3-4   5 minutes

Tofu dip is made with salty doenjang and various seasonings such as sesame oil and spring onions (scallions). It is creamy, savoury and a lighter alternative to traditional mayonnaise-based dips. Serve with fresh vegetables, crackers or chips (fries).

INGREDIENTS
150g (5½oz) firm tofu
150g (5½oz) doenjang
100g (3½oz) onion, finely chopped
Handful of walnuts, crushed
1 tablespoon sesame oil
1 tablespoon toasted sesame seeds

1. Drain the tofu and mash it completely in a bowl.

2. Add the doenjang, onion, walnuts and sesame oil and gently mix to combine.

3. Sprinkle with sesame seeds. You can use immediately or store the dip in the refrigerator for 2–3 days.

ABOVE, TOFU DOENJANG DIP, PAGE 157

BELOW, GOCHUJANG SAUCE, PAGE 156

초간장

KOREAN SOY SAUCE VINEGAR DIP

CHO-GANGJANG

Serves 3-4 3 minutes

A popular dipping sauce for Korean savoury pancakes or *jeon* (see pages 138, 141 and 142). This is a vinaigrette made with soy sauce, rice vinegar and onion. This dip is incredibly versatile and can be used to dress salads or drizzle over stir-fried vegetables.

INGREDIENTS

3 tablespoons soy sauce
3 tablespoons rice vinegar (or white wine vinegar)
1 tablespoon honey (or maple syrup)
2 tablespoons water
½ onion, finely chopped

1. Whisk the ingredients together in a bowl until well combined. Taste and adjust the seasoning by adding soy sauce if you desire a saltier flavor or vinegar if you prefer more acidity.

2. Use immediately or store in a sealed container in the refrigerator for up to a week.

초고추장

GOCHUJANG VINAIGRETTE

CHO-GOCHUJANG

Serves 3-4 3 minutes

Gochujang vinaigrette is a great way to add some Korean-inspired flavours to your dishes and is particularly well-suited to salads, noodles, seafood and sashimi.

INGREDIENTS

40g (1½oz) gochujang
2 tablespoons soy sauce
2 tablespoons rice vinegar (or white wine vinegar)
2 tablespoons sugar
1 tablespoon lemon juice
1 tablespoon sesame oil
½ tablespoon minced garlic
½ tablespoon toasted sesame seeds

1. Simply whisk everything together in a bowl or jar until smooth. The result is a smooth dressing with a fiery kick that adds depth and complexity to any dish.

2. Use immediately or store in a sealed container in the refrigerator for up to a month.

DRINKS & SWEETS

술, 스윗트

9

Koreans don't typically gravitate towards sugary confections for dessert. Instead, we go for naturally sweet stuff like watermelon, persimmons, apples and oranges for a wholesome end to a meal, or for a creamy shaved ice dessert known as *bingsoo*, topped with all kinds of sweet treats, such as mango (see page 168). And, of course, soju, a Korean clear spirit that can be consumed neat or in a cocktail, such as my take on a fruit punch, which combines soju with refreshing watermelon (see page 165).

Get your soju cocktail game on! Here's a simple recipe to get you started. Mix 1 part soju with a splash of your favourite drink, and voilà! A delicious, refreshing cocktail that's perfect for any occasion.

수박소주

WATERMELON SOJU PUNCH

SUBAK SOJU

Serves 4–5   15 minutes

INGREDIENTS
1 medium watermelon
350ml (12fl oz) soju
330ml (11fl oz) lemonade
Sugar (optional)
Ice cubes

In Korea, summers are long and hot. One way to beat the heat is by enjoying thirst-quenching fruits served chilled as ice-infused punches. This delightful concoction pairs refreshing watermelon with soju: perfect for cooling down on a hot day or for a dinner party.

1. Cut open the watermelon and scoop all the flesh from the skin, discarding any seeds. If you have a melon baller, make 4–5 watermelon balls and reserve as garnish.

2. Transfer the watermelon flesh to a blender and add the soju and lemonade. Blend to a smooth juice. Taste and add sugar if needed.

3. Serve over ice with a skewered ball of watermelon in the glass.

D
R
I
N
K
S

&

S
W
E
E
T
S

소맥

SOJU & BEER BOMB

SOMAEK

Serves 1   2 minutes

D
R
I
N
K
S

&

S
W
E
E
T
S

The Soju Bomb, or as it's known in Korean, *somaek*, is an after-hours favourite: a perfect blend of soju and beer, with the golden ratio being 3 parts soju to 7 parts beer. The more soju you add, the stronger your drink will be, but for the perfect balance, stick with the golden 3:7 ratio.

INGREDIENTS
210ml (7fl oz) beer
90ml (3fl oz) soju

1. Grab a pint glass and pour in the beer. Add in the soju and mix well. It's that simple!

야쿠르트 소주

YAKULT® SOJU PUNCH

Serves 2–3   2 minutes

This drink was popular around universities around 20 years ago, but is now having a renaissance among many young people. The golden ratio for this tasty cocktail is 4:2:1 of soju:Yakult®:lemonade. It's very drinkable, you will see why it's so popular!

INGREDIENTS
400ml (13½fl oz) soju
200ml (7fl oz) Yakult®
100ml (3½fl oz) lemonade or soda water
Ice cubes

1. Half-fill a large jug (pitcher) with ice, then add the soju, Yakult® and lemonade and gently stir.

깻잎 모히토

KOREAN-STYLE MOJITO

Serves 1

5 minutes

This is a Korean-style twist on the classic Cuban Mojito, using perilla leaves and soju in place of mint leaves and white rum. It is a refreshing, sophisticated cocktail that offers a perfect balance of sweet and tart flavours which goes very well with Korean food or other Asian dishes and is perfect for a summer barbecue. If you can't find fresh perilla, use mint leaves instead.

INGREDIENTS
1–2 fresh perilla leaves or 8–10 mint leaves, plus extra to garnish
¼ lime, cut into small pieces
70ml (2½fl oz) soju
Ice cubes
70ml (2½fl oz) lemonade
Thinly sliced cucumber, to garnish

1. Put the perilla or mint leaves and lime pieces in a tall glass, then use a muddler (or wooden spoon) to muddle the leaves and lime to release their oils and juices.

2. Next, add the soju to the glass and mix well. Fill the glass with ice cubes and top it up with the lemonade for a bubbly finish.

3. Give the drink a good stir and garnish with sliced cucumber and perilla leaves for a vibrant and Instagram-worthy presentation.

김치 칵테일

KIMCHI BLOODY MARY

Serves 1

5 minutes

This spicy, tangy cocktail combines the classic ingredients of a Bloody Mary with the kick of kimchi.

INGREDIENTS
70ml (2½fl oz) soju
200ml (7fl oz) kimchi brine
100ml (3½fl oz) tomato juice
2 tablespoons lemon juice
½ teaspoon sugar syrup
Ice cubes

To garnish
Lemon and lime wedge
Sliced kimchi
Sliced red and green (bell) pepper

1. Simply combine the ingredients in a shaker. Shake it up, strain it into a pint glass and fill to the brim with fresh ice!

2. Garnish your cocktail with a lemon and a lime wedge, and a skewer of sliced kimchi, red and green (bell) pepper.

망고빙수

MANGO SHAVED ICE

MANGO BIGSOO

Serves 2

5 minutes plus freezing

D
R
I
N
K
S

&

S
W
E
E
T
S

Shaved ice or *bingsoo* is a favourite Korean dessert, consisting of finely shaved frozen milk topped with an array of toppings from sweet red beans (the original, known as *pat-bingsoo*) to fruits and syrups. In recent times, the mango version has taken centre stage – the perfect combination of a fluffy, snow-like base crowned with sweet golden mango.

INGREDIENTS

500ml (18fl oz) full-fat (whole) milk
4 tablespoons sweet condensed milk, plus extra to garnish
Pinch of salt
300g (10½oz) fresh (or frozen) mango, cut into bite-sized pieces

1. Combine the milk, condensed milk and salt in a bowl. Transfer the mixture to a zip-seal bag and place flat in the freezer. Freeze overnight or for at least 5 hours.

2. Once the mixture has frozen, bash it roughly to break it up.

3. Serve in dessert glasses, topped with mango chunks and drizzled with condensed milk. Enjoy!

검은깨두부 아이스크림

TOFU ICE CREAM WITH BLACK SESAME SEEDS

Serves 2

5 minutes plus freezing

This is dairy-free treat that is perfect for vegans and non-vegans alike: ice cream made with classic Korean flavours, tofu and sesame. You can use any milk for this but I like almond best as it complements the nutty taste of sesame.

INGREDIENTS

150g (5½oz) firm tofu
75ml (5 tablespoons) dairy-free milk alternative, such as almond milk
2 tablespoons toasted black sesame seeds, plus extra to garnish
1 tablespoon sugar
Pinch of salt
Sesame oil, to serve

1. Put all the ingredients except the sesame oil in a blender and blitz until smooth.

2. Transfer the mixture to a wide freezer-proof container and place in the freezer for at least 3 hours.

3. Once the mixture has frozen, give it another quick blitz it a blender.

4. Scoop the tofu ice cream into serving bowls and drizzle a touch of sesame oil and sprinkle with extra sesame seeds on top.

된장 카라멜 쿠키

DOENJANG SALTED CARAMEL COOKIES

These cookies offer a unique twist on the traditional salted caramel flavour. The salty essence of doenjang, the sweetness of caramel and the nuttiness of sesame seeds work perfectly together. If you love sweet and salty flavours, these chewy cookies are perfect – and they are super-easy to make. Enjoy them warm from the oven.

12
Makes 12

10 minutes plus chilling

15 minutes

INGREDIENTS

100g (3½oz) unsalted butter
140g (5oz) caster (superfine) sugar
1 egg yolk, at room temperature
50g (1¾oz) doenjang
240g (8½oz) plain (all-purpose) flour
½ teaspoon baking powder
150g (5½oz) toasted black sesame
 seeds
80g (2¾oz) caramel sauce (or
 chopped toffee pieces)

1. Beat the butter and sugar in a large mixing bowl until fluffy and light. Add the egg yolk and doenjang and mix until well combined.

2. Gradually add the flour, baking powder, sesame seeds and caramel sauce to the mix. Stir gently to combine to form a soft dough.

3. Using your hands, shape the dough into small rounds, about 4–5cm (2in) across and 1cm (½in) thick. Place them, spaced apart, on a baking tray lined with baking paper. Cover the tray in clingfilm and refrigerate for 10–15 minutes until the dough becomes firm.

4. While the dough is chilling, preheat the oven to 160°C fan/350°F/gas mark 4.

5. Remove the clingfilm and bake the cookies for 7 minutes, then reduce the oven temperature to 140°C fan/325°F/gas mark 3 and bake for a further 5 minutes.

6. Serve the cookies warm to enjoy the molten caramel centres.

☺ SEJI'S TIP
If you're in the mood for subtle spiciness, consider using gochujang instead of doenjang.

INDEX

THANK YOU

I'd like to thank to my mom Jooyoung and my other family members for their emotional support throughout the twists and turns of the past year.

In particular, I'd like to big thank you to all my friends in London – Sue, Minkyung, Mieun, Nicki, Heidi, Amy, Katy, Louise and Fiona. You have played a significant role in enriching the recipes in this book through your recipe testing, valuable feedback, and spiritual guidance.

Also, thank you to my team at BOMBOM – Sophie, Jules and June!!!

A special thank you to Samhita and Yasia at Octopus Publishing and Kyle Books. A huge shoutout is reserved for Louise and Jake, the creative forces behind bringing our book to life. Your dedication is genuinely appreciated.

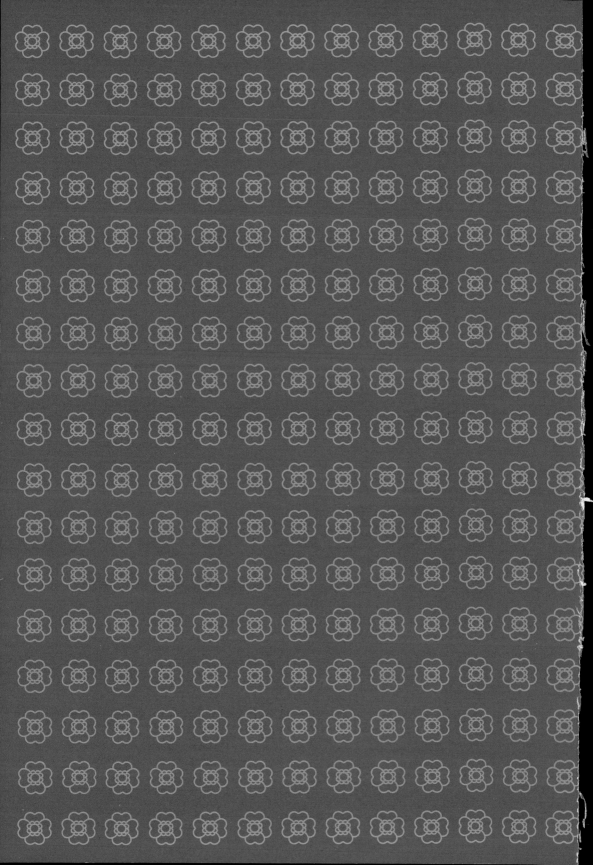